D1173004

Library of Congress Cataloging-in-Publication Data

Plitt, Amy.
  Subway adventure guide: New York City : to the end of the line / Amy Plitt, Kyle Knoke.
    pages cm
  ISBN 978-1-62937-077-4 (paperback)
  1. New York (N.Y.)—Guidebooks. 2. Subways—New York (State)—New York—Guidebooks. I. Knoke, Kyle. II. Title. III. Title: New York City.
  F128.18.P56 2015
  917.47'10444—dc23

                                                                                    2014044055

This book is available in quantity at special discounts for your group or organization. For further information, contact:

Triumph Books LLC
814 North Franklin Street
Chicago, Illinois 60610
(312) 337-0747
www.triumphbooks.com

Printed in U.S.A.
ISBN: 978-1-62937-077-4

Graphics Allen/James Design
Designers Michael Gerwe, Jeni Moore, Alex Schultz
Production Artist Patricia Frey
Creative Director Kyle Knoke
Special Thanks Mark Heavey of the Metropolitan Transportation Authority and Arlene Scanlan of Moxie.

Cover photo courtesy of iStockphoto.com with enhancement from Shane Ramkissoon

© **Arts & Design Collaborative** — Commissioned by Metropolitan Transportation Authority Arts & Design.

- **2** **Wakefield-241 St** Alfredo Ceibal, *Permanent Residents and Visitors,* 2010
- **5** **Eastchester-Dyre Ave** Naomi Campbell, *Animal Tracks,* 2004
- **6** **Pelham Bay Pkwy** Romare Bearden, *City of Glass,* 1993
- **A** **Far Rockaway-Mott Ave** Jason Rohlf, *Respite,* 2011
- **C** **Euclid Ave** Al Loving, *Brooklyn, New Morning,* 2001
- **2 5** **Flatbush Ave-Brooklyn College** Muriel Castanis, *Flatbush Floogies,* 1996
- **A** **Inwood-207th Street** Sheila Levrant De Bretteville, *At the Start... At Long Last,* 1999

Subway Adventure Guide
NEW YORK CITY

Amy Plitt | Kyle Knoke

to the end of the

Contents

To the end of the line.

Whether you're a lifelong New Yorker or simply shuttling around town for a week on vacation, you'll eventually find yourself on the subway. It's an artery connecting different areas of the city; a lifeline that helps people get from point A to point B; and a great equalizer. Not only that, but riding the subway is one of the best ways to get to know the city. And learning the language of the transit maps is, for many, the first step to truly becoming a New Yorker.

But even the most seasoned New Yorkers may not have ridden their usual subway to the end of the line. Each end is also a beginning, a point where the train both empties out and fills again. You've probably seen the names of those stations on the subway maps, and maybe even used them as a way to orient yourself while traveling to a destination. But have you ever wondered what's at the end of the M in Middle Village, or what you'll find at the end of the 6 in Pelham Bay Park?

If so, you've come to the right place. With this book, we want to provide a starting point for your own explorations at the ends of New York City's 24 subway lines. We visited those areas by rail and on foot to find the most exciting things to do and the tidbits you may not have known about each place. Each end is slightly quirky in its own way—did you know there are three ends to the A line?—but what they all have in common is the wealth of stories you'll find. To explore New York City as you may never have seen it before, all you need is a MetroCard.

Stay on board. Adventure awaits at the end of the line.

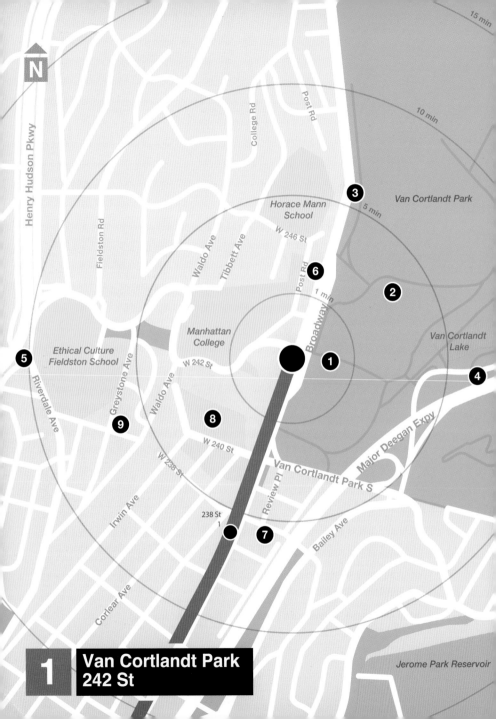

N

15 min

10 min

Van Cortlandt Park

Henry Hudson Pkwy

College Rd

Post Rd

Horace Mann School

3

5 min

Fieldston Rd

W 246 St

Waldo Ave

Tibbett Ave

Post Rd

6

1 min

2

Broadway

Van Cortlandt Lake

Manhattan College

Ethical Culture Fieldston School

Greystone Ave

W 242 St

5

1

4

Riverdale Ave

Waldo Ave

9

8

Major Deegan Expy

W 240 St

W 238 St

Irwin Ave

238 St
1

7

Van Cortlandt Park S

Review Pl

Bailey Ave

Corlear Ave

Jerome Park Reservoir

1 **Van Cortlandt Park
242 St**

to Van Cortlandt Park-242 St

Situated at the crossroads of Riverdale, Kingsbridge, and Fieldston, this subway stop deposits riders into one of the most storied corners of the Bronx. Anchored by Van Cortlandt Park, the third-largest park in the city, the area just off the 1 is full of historic sites and natural attractions; it's also one of the borough's wealthiest enclaves.

The neighborhood dates back to well before Dutch settlers arrived in New York. Glacial activity created the terrain of what later became Van Cortlandt Park, and the Lenape took up residence in the area more than a thousand years ago. Once European settlers arrived, they quickly established some of the landmarks the area is best known for, including the park and the Van Cortlandt House Museum (named for the Van Cortlandt family, who lived there for more than 100 years).

As time progressed, Riverdale became a genteel settlement, while Kingsbridge remained solidly middle-class. Irish immigrants settled in the area (hence the proliferation of pubs and Catholic churches), and in the latter part of the 20th century, the two neighborhoods became more diverse. Fieldston, a hamlet close to the park, is one of the Bronx's richest enclaves, and home to tony institutions like Horace Mann School and the Ethical Culture Fieldston School.

To see these historical areas for yourself, take the 1 to the end of the line. You'll exit right into Van Cortlandt Park, but be sure to wander the quiet streets, which seem like something out of a storybook rather than the Bronx.

to Van Cortlandt Park-242 St

1 **Van Cortlandt Park.** Set on more than 1,000 acres, this massive park is one of the city's best-preserved natural spaces. There are miles of trails, natural forest, and wetlands.

2 **Van Cortlandt House Museum.** Built in 1748, this stone structure is the oldest house in the Bronx. It was built by Frederick Van Cortlandt for his family, and now holds artifacts from New York's earliest days.

3 **Tortoise and the Hare statue.** This sculpture has been a marker on Van Cortlandt Park's three-mile cross-country track since 1997, alluding to the fable about the slow and steady tortoise and the too-quick hare.

4 **Van Cortlandt Park Golf Course.** Yes, there's a golf course in the middle of the Bronx: "Vanny" (the local nickname) opened in 1895, and has been a popular spot for tee time ever since.

5 **Bell Tower Park.** The heart of this small park is a 50-foot stone tower designed by architect Dwight James Baum. It was erected in 1930 and dedicated to World War I veterans.

6 **Jake's Steakhouse.** A former sports bar-turned-chophouse, Jake's offers solid renditions of classic steakhouse dishes: wedge salad, filet mignon topped with blue cheese, and creamed spinach, to name a few.

7 **Bronx Alehouse.** Yes, you can watch football and basketball at this pub, but it's no mere sports bar: delicious pub grub (try the nachos) and an oft-rotating draft list elevate it to the ranks of an excellent neighborhood bar.

8 **Gaelic Park.** Harking back to Riverdale's Irish roots, this stadium hosts sporting events (including hurling, a high-speed lacrosse-like game) for the Gaelic Athletics Association, as well as Manhattan College.

9 **An Beal Bocht Cafe.** This convivial Irish pub is one of the neighborhood's best spots for live music, a pint (try the house beer, Le Chéile), and a comforting plate of grub, like bangers and mash.

1

5

FACTS
OFF THE

1

1. As a small child, President John F. Kennedy lived in a house on Independence Avenue and went to Riverdale Country School.

2. Famous non-Presidential Riverdale residents include Carly Simon, Neil DeGrasse Tyson, and Lou Gehrig.

3. Jack Kerouac, who spent a year at Horace Mann, referenced the 242nd Street stop in his seminal novel *On the Road.*

4. Riverdale is among the highest New York City neighborhoods with views of Manhattan.

5. The lake in Van Cortlandt Park is the largest freshwater lake in all of the Bronx.

ALONG THE WAY

● 231 St

● Marble Hill-225 St

Tibbett Diner. The expansive menu at this local favorite encompasses diner classics, Greek specialties, and more.

Marble Hill Avenue. This small street in Manhattan's northernmost neighborhood is full of Victorian-style homes.

| Dyckman St | 191 St | 157 St |

Sherman Creek Park. Rowing clubs gather at the Peter Jay Sharp Boathouse, just one feature of this waterfront park.

Primavera. Artist Raúl Colón created this glass subway mosaic, inspired by the diversity of Washington Heights.

Trinity Cemetery. Ralph Ellison, Jerry Orbach, and Ed Koch are among the famous folks buried at this gravesite.

to Woodlawn

Exit the subway at the end of the 4, and you'll be in a bit of an odd place. Despite its name, the station doesn't sit in the Woodlawn neighborhood; that area's main thoroughfares (Katonah Avenue, McLean Avenue) are a solid mile from the end of the line.

The neighborhood and the subway stop actually take their name from Woodlawn Cemetery, a 400-acre gravesite that abuts Van Cortlandt Park to the west, and Bronx Park to the east. The cemetery opened in 1863, and its first famous resident—Admiral David Farragut, a naval officer who fought in the Civil War—was interred there in 1870. Since then, a veritable who's-who of famous New Yorkers have chosen to spend eternity there, including newspaper publisher Joseph Pulitzer and jazz legend Max Roach.

The cemetery is bordered to the south by the neighborhood of Norwood, home to Montefiore Medical Center and Williamsbridge Oval. (For more on that, see page 22.) Woodlawn, to the north, is colloquially known as Little Ireland, with Katonah Avenue in particular crowded with Gaelic pubs, shops, and restaurants.

That section of Woodlawn might be a bit of a hike from the end of the line, but considering all that you'll see along the way—many of the neighborhood's best attractions are within the cemetery—it's worth the trek, especially since a perfectly poured pint of Guinness awaits you at the end.

to Woodlawn

1 **Woodlawn subway station.** The Woodlawn station opened here in 1918. Squire Vickers, one of the system's original architects, designed the stop in the Arts and Crafts style.

2 **Woodlawn Cemetery.** The list of notables who chose Woodlawn as their final resting place is impressive: Celia Cruz, Miles Davis, former mayor Fiorello LaGuardia, Herman Melville, and Duke Ellington among them.

3 **Woodlawn Conservancy Tours.** To see the mausoleums and famous graves at Woodlawn, take a public tour through this group, which hosts themed excursions (including nighttime tours), music performances, and more.

4 **Woodlawn Lake.** Take a stroll around this pretty body of water, located toward the northern end of the cemetery; there are mausoleums around it, and bridges along the way.

5 **The Woolworth Chapel.** Located on the cemetery grounds, this small sanctuary is a bright, airy spot for services and the occasional public event. It's named for the Woolworth family, members of which are buried at Woodlawn.

6 **Mosholu-Pelham Greenway.** This miles-long pathway connects Van Cortlandt Park to Bronx Park and beyond via—you guessed it—Mosholu Parkway. There are bike paths and walking trails, as well as a World War I memorial.

7 **Billy's Rochambeau Restaurant.** Located on a tiny, one-block street just south of the cemetery, this eatery (named for its chef and the street it's on) serves hearty Jamaican curries, rice dishes, and more.

8 **The Rambling House.** Pass an evening at this Irish pub with a pint of Smithwick's or Guinness, and you'll fit right in. Hearty classics like shepherd's pie and bangers and mash are on offer, and bands play every night.

9 **Prime Cuts Irish Butchers.** If you're looking for Emerald Isle specialties like corned beef or blood pudding, look no further. The shop also sells Irish chocolates, jams, soda bread, and other traditional treats.

1. *Titanic* victims Isidor and Ida Straus have a memorial at Woodlawn Cemetery; fittingly, it's shaped like a ship.

2. Famous architects, including the firms of McKim, Mead & White, and Carrère and Hastings, created pieces within the cemetery.

3. The neighborhood is referred to as both Woodlawn and Woodlawn Heights (which you'll see on some street signs).

4. In 2002, artist Patricia Cronin installed a Neoclassical sculpture of her and her wife on a plot she bought at Woodlawn.

5. At the start of *The Warriors*, the gang runs through a cemetery that's meant to be Woodlawn, but was actually filmed in Queens.

ALONG THE WAY

● Mosholu Pkwy   ● Bedford Park Blvd

Bronx High School of Science.
Alums from this storied school
include Nobel and Pulitzer Prize
winners...and Jon Favreau.

Jerome Park. The reservoir at
this park's center was drained
in 2008, but may be filled again
within a few years.

Kingsbridge Rd ●   **Fordham Rd** ●   **161 St-Yankee Stadium** ●

Kingsbridge Armory. The huge, historic armory is in the process of being turned into an ice-skating rink and center.

Saint James Episcopal Church. This landmark has windows by Louis Comfort Tiffany, including a replica of *The Last Supper*.

Yankee Stadium. Of all of NYC's sports teams, the Bronx Bombers, who play here, are the most iconic.

N

Mosholu Pkwy
4

8

Bainbridge Ave

E Gun Hill Rd

Grand Concourse

East Mosholu Pkwy

9

Reservoir Oval

4

5

Perry Ave

Bedford Park
Blvd- Lehman
College
4

7

6

Decatur Ave

1 min

Mosholu Pkwy

Bedford Park Blvd
B-D

Hull Ave

E 204 St

Webster Ave

5 min

Bainbridge Ave

Marion Ave

Bronx Blvd

Bronx River Pkwy

E 198 St

1

Southern Blvd

Twin Lakes

10 min

Bronx Park Rd

15 min

Thain Family Forest

Webster Ave

2

New York
Botanical Garden

Bronx Park E

20 min

Fordham
University

25 min

E Fordham Rd

D **Norwood
205 St**

3

Bronx Park

35 min

to Norwood-205 St

The terminus of the D train is in the tiny neighborhood of Norwood—an area that's fewer than a square mile in size, but one that's full of interesting historical tidbits.

During the Revolutionary War, Norwood was occupied by British troops, who fought several small battles with American troops in the area. But despite the turmoil, the neighborhood's oldest house, a small stone structure built by Isaac Valentine in 1758, managed to stay put; now, it's home to a museum chronicling the borough's history.

Another piece of the area's history can be found at Williamsbridge Oval, a small park just outside of the subway station. The site was once the Williamsbridge Reservoir, which ferried water to the Bronx for decades. When that particular supply was no longer needed, the land was rehabbed and turned into a park in 1937. But one bit of the old reservoir remains: The Keeper's House, across the street from the park, became a national historic site in 1999.

The triangle-shaped neighborhood happens to be nestled between a plethora of urban oases, including Van Cortlandt Park, Mosholu Parkway's greenway, Woodlawn Cemetery, and Bronx Park. It's just close enough to the latter to put it within walking distance of landmarks like the New York Botanical Garden and the Bronx Zoo (provided you don't mind a leisurely stroll through green spaces to get there).

to Norwood-205 St

1 **Bronx Park.** There's a ton to do in this 718-acre park. Along with the Botanical Garden and Bronx Zoo, it's home to ballfields, natural forests, and the Bronx River, where people can often be found kayaking.

2 **New York Botanical Garden.** With gardens spread out over 250 acres, the Botanical Garden is a verdant haven. Don't miss the annual Holiday Train Show, in which replicas of New York landmarks are rendered in plant form.

3 **Wildlife Conservation Society's Bronx Zoo.** This may not be the city's first zoo, but at 265 acres, it's NYC's largest. Its menagerie includes animals from around the globe, including sea lions, penguins, and baboons.

4 **Williamsbridge Oval.** Built on the former site of the Williamsbridge Reservoir, this small park has a track and hosts sporting events. There are also benches where you can perch above the fray.

5 **Valentine-Varian House.** Bronx farmer Isaac Valentine built this stone dwelling in 1758 (Isaac Varian bought it in 1792, hence the name); now, it houses the Museum of Bronx History.

6 **Nicky's Coffee Shop.** A neighborhood mainstay for decades, Nicky's is a classic Greek diner. The expansive menu offers the usual eggs, burgers, and sandwiches, along with dishes like gyro and a Greek salad.

7 **Sal's Pizzeria.** Despite the name, the menu at this restaurant (opened by Sal Calces in 1980) isn't limited to only pizza. Hearty Italian fare, including fried calamari and baked spaghetti, is also on offer.

8 **Queen of Tacos.** The exterior of this Mexican deli–cum-restaurant may be unassuming, but the specialties found within—including traditional dishes like *chilaquiles*, pozole, and *cemitas*—are delicious.

9 **Bronx County Historical Society.** In addition to the Museum of Bronx History, this organization also operates a research library out of its Bainbridge Avenue headquarters.

D

1. Norwood's name has an incredibly simple backstory: it's likely a combination of "north wood."

2. Two of Norwood's most famous former residents are fashion designers Calvin Klein and Ralph Lauren.

3. At its peak, the Williamsbridge Reservoir could hold more than 100 million gallons of water.

4. Norwood wasn't meant to be the terminus; the proposed "Burke Ave extension" would have taken the D further into the Bronx.

5. Norwood's once-thriving Irish community also called the area "Bainbridge" or "Little Belfast."

Bronx Opera Company. This acclaimed company puts on two productions every year at a Lehman College theater.

Edgar Allan Poe Cottage. In the years before his death, macabre poet Edgar Allan Poe lived in this tiny farmhouse.

● Fordham Rd   ● Tremont Av   ● 167 St

188 Bakery Cuchifritos. Try the namesake fried pork at this Puerto Rican lunch counter.

Richman Park. Also known as "Echo Park," for the way noises echo between the two giant rocks in the space.

Bronx Museum of the Arts. This institution often hosts exhibits and community events aimed at Bronx residents.

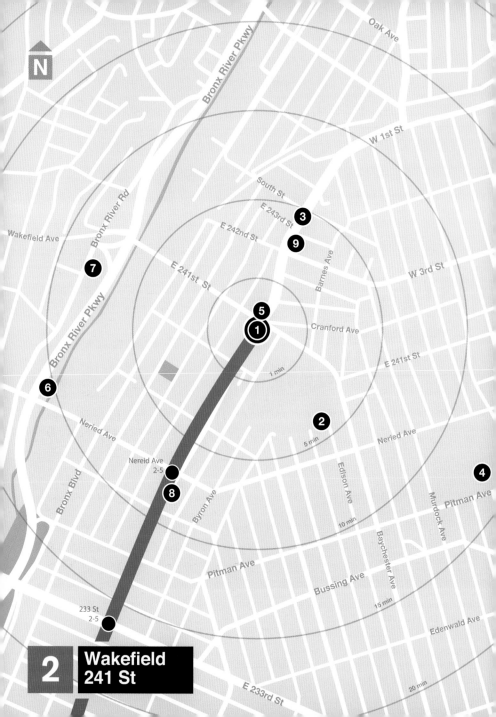

N

Oak Ave

Bronx River Pkwy

W 1st St

South St

E 243rd St **3**

E 242nd St **9**

Bronx River Rd

Wakefield Ave

Barnes Ave

W 3rd St

E 241st St

7

Cranford Ave

5
1

E 241st St

1 min

Bronx River Pkwy

6

2

5 min

Nereid Ave

Neried Ave

Bronx Blvd

Nereid Ave
2-5

Edison Ave

4

Pitman Ave

Murdock Ave

8

Byron Ave

10 min

Baychester Ave

Bussing Ave

Pitman Ave

15 min

233 St
2-5

Edenwald Ave

2 Wakefield
241 St

20 min

E 233rd St

② to Wakefield-241 St

When you reach the end of the 2 in the Bronx, there's no mistaking that you're at the end of line; in fact, one of the MTA's maintenance yards, where trains are held while they're not in service, is located just across the way from the Wakefield–241 St subway station. But Wakefield isn't merely where the 2 ends; it's also one of the ends of the Bronx, with Westchester County within walking distance of the subway station. That means Wakefield can feel, in parts, like more of a suburb than a New York City borough.

In fact, in its infancy Wakefield wasn't part of New York City at all, but a separate incorporated village. In 1895, the town was annexed to the city (along with Pelham and Eastchester), and it became part of the Bronx when that borough was created in 1898. The neighborhood has historically been a middle-class enclave, attracting Irish and Italian immigrants in the early part of the 20th century, and later seeing an influx of Jamaican, African American, and Hispanic residents.

To see this odd juxtaposition of city and suburb, take the 2 to its terminus. Head south, and you'll be in the Bronx; take a few steps north along White Plains Road (which, ironically, doesn't go all the way to White Plains), and you're in Westchester. You'll know when you've crossed into Mount Vernon by the street signs—they're printed in blue and white, not the normal green and white used by the city of New York.

to Wakefield-241 St

(1) *Permanent Residents and Visitors.* The name of this piece in the Wakefield station alludes to the birds who travel in and out of NYC; artist Alfredo Ceibal rendered ducks, jays, and geese in bits of colored glass.

(2) **Bissel Gardens.** For more than 20 years, neighborhood residents have maintained this two-acre haven, which includes a community garden, a seasonal farmers' market, and a space where kids can learn about nature.

(3) **Bronx County line (243rd St).** Walk a block north of the subway station, and you won't be in New York City anymore; the county line, which divides Westchester and the Bronx, is at about 243rd Street.

(4) **Ripe Kitchen and Bar.** Chef Nigel Spence brings the flavors of his native Jamaica to this Mount Vernon spot—the jerk ribeye steak is good enough to warrant a challenge from Food Network chef Bobby Flay. (Spence won.)

(5) **Peppino's Pizza.** This neighborhood mainstay serves slices, along with other Italian specialties, in a corner space just outside of the Wakefield subway station.

(6) **River's Edge Restaurant.** Just across the Bronx River in Yonkers, this restaurant also doubles as a homey sports bar, offering cheap bar food (wings and sliders) and budget drafts during games.

(7) **Valentino's Restaurant.** For more than 30 years, this family-owned Italian restaurant has been slinging red-sauce classics—lasagna, linguine with clam sauce, and chicken parmigiana—in a cheery Yonkers space.

(8) **HIM Ital Health Food Market.** Vegan explorers would do well to check out this market-restaurant, which offers veg-friendly dishes like pasta or rice salad, stewed lentils, and vegan curries.

(9) **Singh's Sporting Goods.** Ricky Singh's small shop is an excellent spot to learn about cricket, the ball-and-bat sport that's hugely popular around the world. In fact, the national teams from the United States and Bermuda get their equipment from Singh.

5
FACTS
OFF THE

2

1. The Wakefield–241 St station is the northernmost subway station in New York City.

2. Even still, Wakefield isn't the city's northernmost point; that distinction belongs to Riverdale.

3. Not sure how to pronounce Nereid Avenue? It's *neer-ee-id,* allegedly named for those mythical water creatures by a local firehouse.

4. Wakefield is named for George Washington's Virginia home, and neighboring Mount Vernon for his former estate.

5. The subway rail yard shouldn't be confused with the one at 240th Street, which is located in Riverdale and services the 1 line.

ALONG THE WAY

233 St   219 St

2

Arrow Cycle. The same family has owned this bike shop, stocking two-wheelers and accessories, for half a century.

Moodie's Records. This legendary record store stocks thousands of LPs, with an impressive selection of Caribbean music.

Gun Hill Rd

Pelham Pkwy

Freeman St

Williamsbridge Square. The subway stop exits into this small park, which hosts a farmers' market on Wednesdays.

Dukagjini Burek. Try the savory namesake pastry at this Albanian spot; it's filled with meat, cheese, or spinach.

Bronx Music Heritage Center Lab. Get schooled on the borough's musical history through live events and talks.

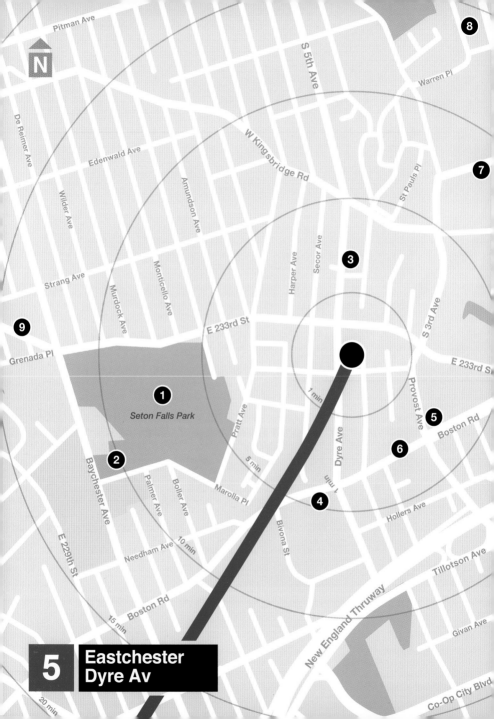

N

Pitman Ave

8

S 5th Ave

Warren Pl

De Reimer Ave

Edenwald Ave

W Kingsbridge Rd

7

St Pauls Pl

Wilder Ave

Amundson Ave

Harper Ave

Secor Ave

3

Strang Ave

Monticello Ave

Murdock Ave

S 3rd Ave

9

E 233rd St

E 233rd St

Grenada Pl

1

Pratt Ave

Seton Falls Park

Provost Ave

5

Boston Rd

Baychester Ave

2

Palmer Ave

Boller Ave

Marolla Pl

Dyre Ave

6

4

E 229th St

Needham Ave

Hollers Ave

Bivona St

Boston Rd

Tillotson Ave

New England Thruway

Givan Ave

5 Eastchester
Dyre Av

Co-Op City Blvd

to Eastchester-Dyre Av

Much like the Wakefield–241 St stop to the west, the area around the end of the 5 occupies an odd place in the city. It's at the Bronx's northeastern tip, with the line separating it from Westchester County (and the town of Mount Vernon) just a few steps away from the train station.

The subway serves the neighborhoods of Eastchester, which lies closer to Pelham Bay Park, and Edenwald, west of the subway stop. Also like the neighborhood of Wakefield, Eastchester was part of its own incorporated town, and was annexed to New York City in 1895. (But a town called Eastchester still exists—it's about five miles north of the Bronx, in Westchester County. Confusing, we know.) Edenwald, meanwhile, includes Seton Falls Park and the Edenwald Houses, the borough's largest housing development. Both neighborhoods are largely working class, with small family homes lining quiet streets.

Because of its place at the juncture of city and county, the area around the end of the subway can feel a little underdeveloped. The main thoroughfares of Boston Road and 233rd Street are filled with auto body shops, small restaurants, and a few chains. Cross the line into Mount Vernon, and you'll find a national park (at Saint Paul's Church), even more shops, and the Hutchinson River.

to Eastchester-Dyre Av

① Seton Falls Park. At the park's western edge, you'll find the man-made stone waterfall that gave it its name; "Seton" refers to the once-prominent family who built the water formation.

② High Rock Playground. Located within Seton Falls Park, this small playground offers plenty of amenities for kids, including a basketball court and a jungle gym. It's also close to the park's nature trail.

③ P.S. 15. Colloquially known as "the Little Red Schoolhouse," this beautiful old building originally opened in 1877, but stopped housing students about a century later. It became a national historic landmark in 1978.

④ Pimento Caribbean Restaurant. Jamaican cuisine is the specialty at this Eastchester restaurant. Try traditional dishes like beef patties, goat curry, and—for the adventurous—cow-foot soup.

⑤ Cozy Cottage. This unassuming diner packs a punch with its huge menu, including Greek dishes, diner favorites (try the disco fries), and Italian sandwiches (like a veal cutlet parmigiana).

⑥ Boston Road. Contrary to the name, this thoroughfare wasn't linked to the historic Boston Post Road; still, it eventually intersects with that Revolutionary lane once you're in Westchester.

⑦ Saint Paul's Church National Historic Site. Cross the county line into Mount Vernon to visit this storied church, once used as a military hospital and visited by presidents like George Washington and Franklin D. Roosevelt.

⑧ Royal Caribbean Bakery. Jamaican couple Vincent and Jeanette HoSang opened this eatery in 1978, and have been serving the dishes of their homeland—including excellent Jamaican patties—ever since.

⑨ Jackie's West Indian Bakery. You'll find more Caribbean specialties at this small bakery, but it's known for doing one thing—coco bread—extremely well. Get it stuffed with jerk chicken or cheese.

5

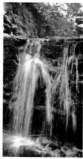

5

FACTS
OFF THE

5

1. Rombouts Avenue, which ends in Eastchester, was named for Francis Rombouts, the 12th mayor of New York City.

2. The subway station was originally built to be used as a stop on the New York, Westchester and Boston Railway.

3. Seton Falls Park shares a name with Elizabeth Ann Seton, the first American to be canonized as a saint.

4. Edenwald gets its name from a palatial estate built by John H. Eden; the land was eventually turned into the housing project.

5. Thanks to the high school named for composer John Philip Sousa near Seton Falls Park, locals often call the green space Sousa Park.

5

Haffen Park. Named for the first Bronx Borough President, this park is home to one of the Bronx's swimming pools.

Nick's Pizza. No-frills, New York-style slices are on the menu at this pizza joint; the Sicilian is also worth a try.

Pelham Pkwy   E 180 St   West Farms Sq-E Tremont Av

Bronx and Pelham Parkway. As the name suggests, this strip of green land connects Bronx Park to Pelham Bay Park.

E 180 St Station. The ornate, Spanish-style entrance to this stop was originally a train depot, and got a $66 million facelift in 2013.

Animal Tracks. Colorful mosaics of giraffes, zebras, and other animals evoke the nearby Bronx Zoo.

N

Bartow Ave

Co-Op City Blvd

New England Thruway

Hutchinson River Pkwy

35 min

Orchard Beach Rd

⑤

③

②
45 min

⑨

25 min

Pelham Bay Park

Givan Creek

City Island Rd

Pelham Bridge Rd

15 min

Turtle Cove

Erskine Pl

5 min

Burr Ave

St Paul Ave

1 min

④

①

Hutchinson River

Wilkinson

⑥

Pelham Bay Park
Nature Center

Edison Ave

Hobart Ave

Parkview Ave

Mahan Ave

Jarvis Ave

Middletown Rd

Ohm Ave

Ampere Ave

Watt Ave

⑧

⑦

6 Pelham Bay Park

to Pelham Bay Park

There's no mistaking where you are once you get to the end of the 6. Not only is the station named for Pelham Bay Park, but when you exit the subway stop, you'll be right in the middle of that expansive space. But the park isn't the only attraction in Pelham Bay—the rest of this quaint neighborhood is worth investigating, too.

The area is named for Thomas Pell, an Englishman who settled the area in the 17th century. Not much else happened in the area—a Revolutionary War battle here, construction of the Bartow-Pell Mansion there—until the late 19th century, when the city bought the land that now makes up Pelham Bay Park and established a public space there. Many of the area's most famous attractions were built soon thereafter; the golf courses, Orchard Beach, several monuments, and more all opened by the mid-20th-century.

Nearby Pelham Bay began to develop once the 6 came to the area in 1920. The neighborhood historically had a large Italian population, and many bakeries and red-sauce joints remain. In recent years, the community has not only become more diverse, but has also welcomed yoga studios and juice bars alongside the old-school businesses.

Pelham Bay is also close, relatively speaking, to City Island, a tiny maritime community on the Long Island Sound that's both intensely small-town—there are only about 4,000 residents—and a tourist magnet. It's worth taking a day (or more) to see everything this nature-filled area has to offer.

to Pelham Bay Park

1   **Pelham Bay Park.** New York City's largest park—it's three times the size of Central Park—occupies more than 2,500 acres, and has hiking trails, wide-open spaces, and playgrounds to explore.

2   **Orchard Beach.** This mile-long stretch of sand faces Long Island Sound; its promenade and bathhouse (the latter is no longer in use) are the work of Robert Moses, who envisioned the space as "the Riviera of New York."

3   **Bartow-Pell Mansion Museum.** This stately manor was built in the 19th century, and turned into a museum in 1946. While the home itself—a stone edifice with Greek Revival touches—is lovely, don't miss the gardens.

4   **Bronx Victory Column.** For this ornate World War I memorial, which was dedicated in 1933, a bronze sculpture of Winged Victory is perched atop an enormous Corinthian column. The entire thing is more than 100 feet tall.

5   **Pelham Bay & Split Rock Golf Course.** These two courses—which opened in 1901 and 1936, respectively—now operate under one umbrella, providing various terrains against Pelham Bay Park's beautiful backdrop.

6   **Giovanni's Restaurant & Pizza.** The menu at this old-school Italian joint covers all the bases: antipasti platters, spaghetti (mix it up with the broccoli rabe and sausage), pizzas, and cutlets, among other specialties.

7   **George's Restaurant.** You can't miss the bright-green awning of this diner, a Pelham Bay staple for decades. Homey fare, including Greek dishes (gyro, Greek salad) and breakfast all day, is on offer.

8   **Zeppieri & Sons.** Since 1968, this family-run Italian bakery has been serving delicious sweets, including traditional desserts like tiramisu and rainbow cake, along with fresh-baked bread.

9   **Bronx Equestrian Center.** Saddle up at this riding facility, where wannabe cowboys can take horseback-riding lessons, or go on meandering walks through Pelham Bay Park. There are also pony rides available for little cowpokes.

5 FACTS OFF THE 6

1. *The Taking of Pelham One Two Three* uses the Pelham Bay Park station as the setting—in the story, the titular train departs at 1:23 PM.

2. The Hutchinson River was named for Anne Hutchinson, who lived near Long Island Sound and was killed by a Native American tribe.

3. In late spring, Orchard Beach becomes overrun with horseshoe crabs, which mate on the beach. (Charming.)

4. Humphrey Bogart was among the soldiers who trained at a naval base in Pelham Bay Park during World War I.

5. Bartow-Pell was once used by Mayor Fiorello LaGuardia as an office, and his staffers took the 6 train to get there.

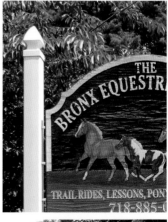

6

Havana Cafe. Traditional Cuban dishes are paired with live events at this spacious restaurant.

City of Glass. Artist Romare Bearden's colorful stained glass panels depict an ever-moving, bustling city.

Castle Hill Av — **Parkchester** — **Whitlock Av**

Neerob. One of the city's best Bangladeshi restaurants serves traditional fare (curries, whole fish) in a friendly environment.

Joe's Place. Chef Joe Torres' menu features Puerto Rican specialties like *arroz con pollo* and *pernil.*

Concrete Plant Park. Once an industrial site, this waterfront park incorporates old concrete silos into its design.

to Court Sq

Long Island City is a neighborhood that's perpetually on the cusp of change. While the Manhattan-facing waterfront area has been revamped in recent years, with sleek high-rises and scenic parks, the area farther inland has been slower to develop—although that may soon change.

Like many of New York City's waterfront neighborhoods, Long Island City was once an industrial hub, with ferries offloading cargo at factories throughout the area. But once its industrial heyday had passed, many of these warehouses were renovated for other uses: The former Silvercup Bakery was converted to Silvercup Studios, where shows like *30 Rock* and *The Sopranos* were filmed, while the Standard Motor Products headquarters became home to the Jim Henson Company and the Franklin Mint.

There's also a long artistic tradition in Long Island City, which thrived thanks to LIC's relative affordability. P.S. 1 Contemporary Art Center (later turned into MoMA PS1) opened in 1976, and the Noguchi Museum followed (in yet another converted factory) in 1985. The beloved 5 Pointz Aerosol Arts Center attracted street artists to a warehouse underneath the subway; unfortunately, it was razed in 2014 to make room for luxury buildings, an all-too-common story in artsy NYC neighborhoods.

The end of the G line lets out at Court Square, an area that's notable mostly for the hulking Citigroup building and its proximity to the Long Island City courthouse (although residential developments are on the way). But Court Square is within walking distance of the best of Long Island City, including new restaurants, its arts scene, and the waterfront.

to Court Sq

(1) MoMA PS1. Housed in a red brick former schoolhouse, this museum hosts innovative contemporary art exhibits. In the summer, its Warm Up parties draw New Yorkers of all stripes to dance in its open courtyard.

(2) Gantry Plaza State Park. Stunning views of the Manhattan skyline aren't the only draw of this waterfront park. It's also home to Long Island City's iconic Pepsi-Cola sign, a symbol of the neighborhood's industrial past.

(3) Dutch Kills Bar. You could sample one of the many cocktails on the menu at this speakeasy, whose name comes from an old moniker for LIC, or let the bartender make a drink for you based on your flavor preferences.

(4) SculptureCenter. This arts institution has been around since 1928, but only moved to its current location—a onetime trolley-repair shop—in 2001. The recently revamped space showcases large-scale and site-specific pieces.

(5) John Brown Smokehouse. Opened in 2012 by a Missouri native, this BBQ joint specializes in Kansas City-style smoked meat. Try the burnt ends for a bit of traditional KC 'cue, paired with sides like coleslaw or cornbread.

(6) LIC Flea and Food. The vendors at this waterfront flea market reflect the diversity of Queens: you might find Japanese bubble tea or Texas kolaches, not to mention vintage furniture, and hand-made clothing and accessories.

(7) M. Wells Steakhouse. This chophouse from the husband-and-wife team behind M. Wells Dinette offers a bold twist on classic dishes. A thick, juicy burger, for instance, comes with a caveman-esque bone.

(8) Sage General Store. This cozy Jackson Avenue spot, which has been featured on The Food Network, offers comfort food (mac and cheese, cheddar biscuits) alongside fancier options like wood-fired cauliflower pizza.

(9) Elevator Historical Society Museum. One of the city's quirkiest museums, this institution charts the deveopment of elevators in New York City, with artifacts culled from founder Patrick Carrajat's extensive personal collection.

G

4
FACTS
OFF THE

G

1. One Court Square—otherwise known as the Citigroup Building—is the tallest building in Queens.

2. Long Island City is home to the Aviation High School, where students learn airplane maintenance and engineering.

3. Some of the foodstuffs that were produced in Long Island City include Chiclets gum, Hellman's mayonnaise, and fortune cookies.

4. Long Island City is separated from Brooklyn by the Newtown Creek, a heavily polluted waterway that became a Superfund site in 2010.

ALONG THE WAY ●————————●
21 St   Greenpoint Av

The Creek and the Cave. You never know when you'll catch a stand-up legend like Louis C.K. or Colin Quinn at this club.

Karczma Restaurant. Fill up on belly-filling Polish food like pickle soup or pierogies at this Greenpoint mainstay.

Nassau Av

Lorimer St

Broadway

Peter Pan Donuts. Be prepared to line up to try the red velvet doughnuts at this decades-old bakery. They're worth the wait.

City Reliquary Museum. This tiny space holds quirky New York artifacts: postcards, subway tokens, old bottles, and more.

Williamsburg Pizza. Old and new Brooklyn are represented at this pizzeria, with both Margherita and kale pies on its menu.

East River

N

15 min

Luyster Creek

10 min

Shore Blvd

21st Ave

21st Dr

26th St

5 min

20th Ave

9

8

19th St

38th St

2

21st St

4

23rd Dr

Crescent St

27th St

29th St

Steinway St

24th St

23rd Ave

26th St

1 min

7

3

36th St

Ditmars Blvd

38th St

21st Ave

29th St

32nd St

33rd St

5

28th St

23rd Ave

6 1

35th St

24th Ave

Grand Central Pkwy

Astoria Blvd
N-Q

34th St

Grand Central Pkwy

Astoria Blvd N

36th St

Steinway St

St Michael's Cemetery

30 Av
N-Q

25th Ave

N Q **Astoria
Ditmars Blvd**

#

to Astoria-Ditmars Blvd

Astoria has managed to retain the small-town charm that has historically attracted residents there, even as it's experienced the gentrification that has moved in waves across the city. Exit the N or Q line at the Astoria-Ditmars Blvd stop, the terminus for both of those lines, and you'll see the neighborhood's old and new charms.

Astoria was originally settled by William Hallett, an English immigrant who would later have a narrow channel in the East River named for him. The area came into its own in the 19th century, when fur trader Stephen A. Halsey built Astoria up and helped attract the city's affluent set. (Halsey tried to get John Jacob Astor to invest money in the area in exchange for naming it after the prominent millionaire—hence, *Astoria*. It didn't work.)

As time went on, Astoria also became a center for industry. In the late 19th century, the Steinway Piano Company opened a factory in the area—giving *Steinway* Street its name. The nascent movie-making industry also found a foothold there: Kaufman-Astoria Studios originally opened in 1920, and remains in operation to this day—in fact, a backlot was added in 2013 to accommodate even more filming.

Astoria has long been one of the city's most diverse neighborhoods, with enclaves for German, Bangladeshi, Egyptian, and Greek residents. In recent years, younger residents and a thriving LGBT community have also moved into the area, creating a mishmash of cultures that makes Astoria uniquely New York.

to Astoria-Ditmars Blvd

1 **Bohemian Hall.** Raise a glass at the city's oldest *biergarten,* a neighborhood presence since 1910. Wash down Czech-style dumplings with one of several easy-drinking beers on tap, including Staropramen.

2 **Astoria Park.** From the edge of this waterfront park, you can see Manhattan's skyline and the iconic Hell Gate Bridge. In the summer, the Astoria Pool—the city's oldest, built in 1936—is one of the most popular spots.

3 **Taverna Kyclades.** Astoria is teeming with Greek spots, but few draw crowds like this Ditmars mainstay. The wait is worth it for the fresh seafood and Greek delicacies, like stuffed grape leaves and spinach pie.

4 **Singlecut Beersmiths.** Queens' beer renaissance is in full swing, and this brewery is one of the borough's best places to grab a pint. Try the 19-33 Queens Lagrrr!, named for Singlecut's address.

5 **Sal, Kris & Charlie's Deli.** There are plenty of sandwiches available at this deli, but you're here for the Bomb, a massive Italian-American hybrid overflowing with meat, cheese, and toppings. Don't try to eat it all at once.

6 **The Sparrow Tavern.** In contrast to the bustling Bohemian Hall, this homey corner pub attracts a low-key local crowd, who are drawn in by the pub grub (with specials like lamb ribs) and the extensive drink list.

7 **Q.E.D.** Acting as a sort of community hub-cum-performance space, this new venue hosts a diverse roster of events: trivia nights, stand-up comedy, storytelling shows, and even craft workshops.

8 **Agnanti Meze.** This eatery specializes in dishes you might not find at an ordinary Greek diner, like *kalitsounia,* small pies that are popular in Crete, or *baccalao skordalia,* fried salt cod served with garlicky potatoes.

9 **Steinway & Sons Factory.** Steinway pianos are played by the likes of Harry Connick Jr., Billy Joel, and Rufus Wainwright. See how they're made at the company's Astoria factory, where tours are offered every Tuesday (you must reserve in advance).

N Q

1. The Steinway family created a company town for workers near its piano factory, which took up several blocks in the area.

2. Astoria is where the Bunkers lived on *All in the Family,* and the Costanza family lived on *Seinfeld.*

3. The Hell Gate Bridge allegedly inspired Sydney, Australia's larger Harbour Bridge, which opened 16 years after its Queens forebear.

4. The most famous client at Kaufman-Astoria Studios is probably *Sesame Street,* which has filmed there for more than 20 years.

5. Astoria Pool was used as a site for Olympic trials in both 1936 and 1964, thanks to its size and now-defunct diving pool.

ALONG THE WAY

● Astoria Blvd

● 30 Av

Titan Foods. This market carries all the olives, feta, and Greek baked goods and candy you could want.

Petey's Burger. The price is right at this burger joint: a juicy cheeseburger can be had for less than $7.

Broadway

36 Av

39 Av

Astoria Bookshop. In addition to selling books by local authors, this indie shop hosts book clubs and workshops.

Museum of the Moving Image. This institution is a pop-culture junkie's paradise, with exhibits on film, TV, and more.

Flux Factory. This arts nonprofit hosts innovative events and art exhibits by both local and global artists.

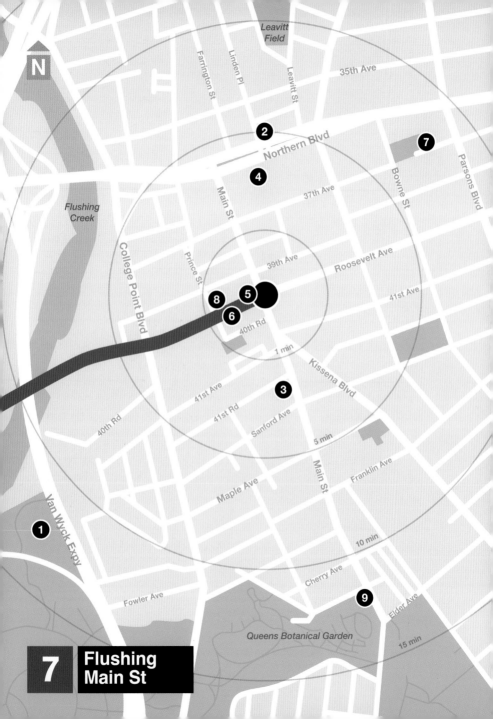

N

Leavitt
Field

35th Ave

Farrington St

Linden Pl

Leavitt St

2

Northern Blvd

4

Main St

37th Ave

Bowne St

Parsons Blvd

7

Flushing
Creek

College Point Blvd

Prince St

39th Ave

Roosevelt Ave

8 **5**

6

40th Rd

41st Ave

1 min

Kissena Blvd

3

41st Ave

41st Rd

Sanford Ave

5 min

40th Rd

Maple Ave

Main St

Franklin Ave

10 min

Van Wyck Expy

1

Fowler Ave

Cherry Ave

9

Elder Ave

15 min

Queens Botanical Garden

7 Flushing
Main St

to Flushing-Main St

If you're passing through Flushing-Main St station, be sure to look up: Ik-Joong Kang's colorful mural *Happy World* hangs over one of the subway turnstiles, providing an apt introduction to the neighborhood. The artwork is made of hundreds of small ceramic tiles that depict scenes of city life, creating a mosaic that reflects Flushing's diverse populace. (Kang said he was inspired to create it by riding the 7 every day.)

That diversity is one of Flushing's most noteworthy traits: According to the 2010 Census data, residents of the neighborhood come from more than 70 countries. The area is best known for being home to one of New York City's largest Chinese communities, but Korean, Indian, and Ecuadoran hubs have all appeared in the neighborhood in recent years, bringing their food, languages, and cultures into the mix.

Flushing is also one of New York City's oldest enclaves, with settlers moving into the area soon after the establishment of New Amsterdam. Some of the city's oldest buildings (including the Quaker Meeting House and the Bowne House, both built in the 1600s) are located there. The Flushing Remonstrance, a document that protested the banishment of the Quaker religion in 17th-century New York, was written there and has since become known as the first expression of freedom of religion in the U.S.

Those two sides—Flushing's present-day diversity and its historic enclaves—make it an ideal destination for exploration. And it all starts from Flushing-Main St, smack in the center of the neighborhood's hustle and bustle, surrounded by tiny eateries, grocery stands, and the sleek Flushing branch of the Queens Library.

to Flushing-Main St

1 **Flushing Meadows–Corona Park.** Spanning 897 acres, this park is home to several Flushing landmarks, including the Unisphere (an iconic symbol of the 1964 World's Fair), Arthur Ashe Stadium, and the Queens Zoo.

2 **Flushing Town Hall.** Housed in a 19th-century Romanesque Revival building, this community center hosts cultural events, workshops, and exhibits, as well as an annual Lunar New Year blowout.

3 **Golden Shopping Mall.** Descend a staircase on packed Main Street to enter this food hub, filled with vendors selling Chinese dishes. It's home to the original Xi'an Famous Foods, known for lip-tingling spicy lamb noodles.

4 **Quaker Meeting House.** This humble building is New York City's oldest house of worship, having fostered a Quaker community since 1694. Visitors can tour the grounds on Sundays, or join a traditionally silent prayer group.

5 **New Flushing Bakery.** Dessert fans will find plenty to love in Flushing, including this pastry haven off the main drag. Try an egg tart, with a sweet custardy base baked in a flaky crust.

6 **Ten Ren Tea & Ginseng.** Not only can you get a refreshing cup of bubble tea at this well-known chain, you can also stock up on fragrant loose-leaf teas.

7 **Queens Historical Society.** Located within the Kingsland Homestead, this institution boasts a large collection of borough-related ephemera. It's adjacent to the Bowne House, one of the oldest landmarks in Queens.

8 **Spicy & Tasty.** You'll find the uniquely spicy flavor of Sichuan cuisine in any number of dishes here, including sautéed dry beef with a peppery red chili sauce, or mapo tofu (bean curd sautéed with spicy minced pork).

9 **Queens Botanical Garden.** Just steps from hectic Main Street, this verdant oasis beckons. Spend a calming day wandering through its many gardens, including ones devoted to herbs, fragrant and colorful blooms, and flora that attracts bees.

1. The "valley of ashes" in F. Scott Fitzgerald's *The Great Gatsby* was inspired by a dump that later became Flushing Meadows.

2. Architect Buckminster Fuller built a geodesic dome for the 1964 World's Fair that can still be seen at the Queens Zoo.

3. In 2013, Flushing-Main St station was the busiest subway stop outside of Manhattan.

4. They Might Be Giants filmed parts of the video for "Don't Let's Start" at the old New York State Pavilion in the park.

5. Famous folks with roots in Flushing include former First Lady Nancy Reagan, composer John Williams, and director Judd Apatow.

ALONG THE WAY

Mets-Willits Point   111 St

7

Citi Field. See the Amazin's (that would be the New York Mets) play at this ballpark, built to replace Shea Stadium in 2009.

Louis Armstrong House Museum. The jazz legend lived at this small house from 1943 until his death.

103 St-Corona Plaza   **Junction Blvd**   **90 St–Elmhurst Av**

Tortilliera Nixtamal. Fresh, warm tortillas made on-site are the anchor of the Mexican specialties here.

Rincon Criollo. This Cuban spot serves traditional fare: *arroz con pollo, ropa vieja,* and creamy flan.

Head east from this stop to sample delicious street food, from Mexican *tortas* to Ecuadorian grilled meats.

N

Mount Olivet
Cemetery

Eliot Ave

Juniper Blvd N

20 min

1

Juniper Valley
Park

71st St

Juniper Blvd S

15 min

2

69th St

Penelope Ave

10 min

69th Pl

Mount Olivet Crescent

5

62nd Ave Crescent

Juniper Valley Rd

3

25 min

66th Rd

74th St

5 min

8 7
6

Metropolitan Ave

Metropolitan Ave

73rd Pl

75th St

1 min

4

Traffic Ave

Lutheran All
Faiths Cemetery

Madison St

9

Joseph F.
Mafera Park

Otto Rd

Fresh Pond Rd
M

Fresh Pond Rd

Central Ave

Cooper Ave

Myrtle Ave

Cypress Hills
Cemetery

M **Middle Village**
Metropolitan Av

to Middle Village-Metropolitan Av

If this particular Queens neighborhood is known for anything, it's the cemetery belt: Of the many cemeteries in Queens, at least three are located in Middle Village, along with a large crematorium that's dealt with the remains of famed athletes, musicians, and other notable New Yorkers. The sleepy community on the Brooklyn-Queens border is the final resting place for thousands of New Yorkers.

So how did Middle Village become cemetery central? The Rural Cemetery Act of 1847 is to thank (or blame, depending on your perspective); its passage made it easier to bury the dead outside of Manhattan, and rural Queens had plenty of space. After burials were outlawed in Manhattan in 1852, even more funerals took place in the borough, and many of Middle Village's cemeteries—including Mt. Olivet and St. John's—were founded around this time. Though Middle Village doesn't quite compare to Cypress Hills to the south, its non-living population is plenty famous, with Geraldine Ferraro, John Gotti, and Robert Mapplethorpe buried there.

Contrary to what all those graveyards might have you think, modern Middle Village isn't a creepy place. It's an otherwise quiet neighborhood, once home to a substantial German community—Niederstein's, a beer hall that was open for 150 years, closed in 2005. It's known for being an area where families tend to live for generations, and things don't change much—and that's how its residents seem to like it.

to Middle Village-Metropolitan Av

① **Juniper Valley Park.** Named for the juniper trees that once covered the land, this park features a roller-hockey rink, jogging track, plenty of open spaces, and—because this is Middle Village—the Pullis Farm Cemetery.

② **Mt. Olivet Cemetery.** One of the oldest cemeteries in Queens, this 71-acre graveyard was founded in 1850. It also has a spooky past: In 1884, a ghost was allegedly spotted here, but couldn't be tracked down.

③ **St. John's Cemetery.** The clientele at this Roman Catholic cemetery includes artist Robert Mapplethorpe, former NYC mayor John Hylan—and a whole lot of mobsters, most famously Lucky Luciano and John Gotti.

④ ***General Slocum* Steamboat Fire Mass Memorial.** This statue honors victims of the *General Slocum* disaster, which killed more than 1,000 people. An annual memorial service has been held every June for more than 100 years.

⑤ **Fresh Pond Crematory and Columbarium.** It may seem weird to take a trip to a crematorium, but there's history here: The building is a Neoclassical gem, *Boardwalk Empire* filmed there, and Notorious B.I.G. was cremated there.

⑥ **Carlo's Pizzeria and Restaurant.** The pizza at this nearly 40-year-old staple is justifiably popular, but don't miss out on the Italian specialties like *arancini* (rice balls) or *scungili*—snails—in marinara sauce.

⑦ **Bella Caracas Cafe.** This colorful Venezuelan joint serves traditional dishes, including arepas (stuffed with everything from avocado and sweet plantain to pulled pork) and *cachapas* (corn cakes with cheese or meat).

⑧ **Ralph's Famous Italian Ices.** The first location of this mini-chain opened on Staten Island in 1928; the Middle Village outpost offers the orange and lemon flavors that Ralph Silvestro first served eight decades ago.

⑨ **Krystal European Bakery.** Run by a Romanian wife-and-husband team, this neighborhood stalwart specializes in Eastern European sweets. Try the strudel, which comes with sweet fillings like apple or cheese.

M

5 FACTS OFF THE M

1. The name Middle Village comes from the neighborhood's location, at the center of the former Williamsburgh and Jamaica Turnpike.

2. Similarly, Fresh Pond Road is so named because of a large pond that once occupied about five acres in the neighborhood.

3. Part of Juniper Valley Park was owned by mobster Arnold Rothstein, notorious for the 1919 Chicago Black Sox scam.

4. Four sections of Middle Village are designated landmark districts, including the area around the VanderEnde Onderdonk House.

5. Middle Village was home to alleged members of the Bonnano and Genovese crime families—not just the ones interred at St. John's.

ALONG THE WAY

● Fresh Pond Rd   ● Forest Av

Antica Trattoria. Old-school Italian-American dishes, including spaghetti carbonara and linguine puttanesca, are on offer.

Gottscheer Hall. A Ridgewood staple for 90 years, this German beer hall serves hearty food and Bavarian beer.

Myrtle-Wyckoff Avs	Central Av	Myrtle Av

This subway stop is fascinating in itself: part of it is located in Brooklyn, and the other part in Queens.

Bossa Nova Civic Club. Boogie at this Bushwick club, where tropical drinks (including a margarita riff) keep partiers moving.

Silent Barn. One of the city's remaining DIY spaces, this venue hosts up-and-coming bands, art exhibits, and other cool events.

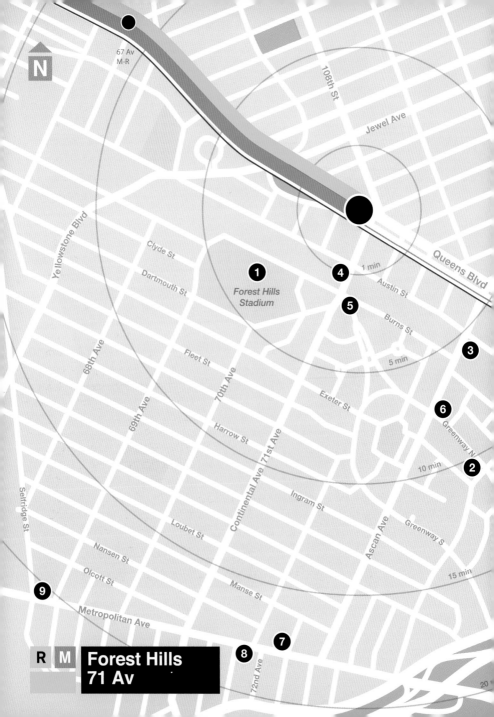

N

67 Av
M-R

108th St

Jewel Ave

Queens Blvd

Clyde St

Dartmouth St

1

*Forest Hills
Stadium*

4

1 min

Austin St

5

Burns St

3

Yellowstone Blvd

68th Ave

Fleet St

70th Ave

5 min

Exeter St

6

Greenway N

69th Ave

Harrow St

Continental Ave 71st Ave

10 min

2

Seitridge St

Loubet St

Ingram St

Ascan Ave

Greenway S

Nansen St

Olcott St

Manse St

15 min

9

Metropolitan Ave

7

8

72nd Ave

R **M** **Forest Hills
71 Av**

20

to Forest Hills-71 Av

You might not expect to find quaint, red-brick Tudor homes on manicured lawns in the middle of Queens, but that's exactly what you'll encounter in Forest Hills. The neighborhood, situated just north of Forest Park (hence the name), feels more like a sleepy suburb than part of New York City.

That's partially due to Forest Hills Gardens, a planned community that was founded in 1909. Its wide roads and pastoral setting seem incongruous with the rest of the city; the development even seems a little out of place with the rest of Forest Hills, where modest homes are the norm. But the Gardens are still an integral part of the neighborhood: the West Side Tennis Club originated there, and notable New Yorkers like columnist Jimmy Breslin (not to mention Spider-Man, allegedly) called it home.

Speaking of noteworthy New Yorkers, the greater Forest Hills area was home to some of the most iconic musicians of the last century; a list of alumni from Forest Hills High School alone includes punk-rock legends the Ramones, folk duo Simon and Garfunkel, and songwriter Burt Bacharach. Actors Hank Azaria and Ray Romano are also neighborhood natives, contributing even further to the area's rish cultural legacy.

The R deposits riders right into the heart of Forest Hills, close to the tennis stadium, the main shopping drag of Austin Street, and Station Square, where President Theodore Roosevelt once delivered a speech. It's an excellent starting point from which to explore the neighborhood.

to Forest Hills-71 Av

1 **Forest Hills Stadium.** Once known for its big-name events—including two Beatles concerts—this venue closed in the '80s. Preservationists helped it reopen in 2013, and it's since hosted Mumford & Sons and the Replacements.

2 **Forest Hills Gardens.** You'll barely recognize this planned community as part of New York City; the large Tudor homes and well-manicured lawns wouldn't look out of place in the English countryside.

3 **Nick's Pizza.** A relative newcomer to NYC's pizza scene—it opened in 1993—Nick's stands out thanks to its gas-cooked pies. Sample the best of both with a half-red, half-white pie—and don't miss the luscious cannoli.

4 **Station House.** Craft beer is the star of the show at this homey pub, with a well-curated list of more than 15 brews. Choose a pint from a Queens-based brewer like Finback or Singlecut Beersmiths.

5 **Station Square.** If Forest Hills has a town square, it's this leafy, quaint space. It's anchored by the red-brick LIRR station, where President Theodore Roosevelt delivered his so-called "unification speech" in 1917.

6 **The Church-in-the-Gardens.** This century-old stone church, listed on the National Register of Historic Places, hosts live music and community meetings along with its normal services.

7 **Eddie's Sweet Shop.** From the neon SODA sign to the marble counter, this shop is the epitome of an old-school parlor. Indulge your sweet tooth with sundaes, milk shakes, and malteds, featuring house-made ice-cream.

8 **Danny Brown Wine Bar & Kitchen.** This Michelin-starred restaurant might offer one of the best deals in the city: every Tuesday and Wednesday, you can partake in the $30 prix-fixe menu.

9 **Royal Collectibles.** Comic books aren't the only collectibles sold at this store; the owners also stock sports memorabilia, action figures, and other pop-culture tchotchkes.

R M

1. From 1924 to 1977, the US Open was held in Forest Hills, at the West Side Tennis Club stadium.

2. The streets in Forest Hills are arranged in alphabetical order, beginning with Austin Street and ending at Olcott Street.

3. After former vice presidential candidate Geraldine Ferraro passed away, the corner of Austin Street and Ascan Avenue was named for her.

4. One of the monuments in Forest Hills Gardens is the mast of the *Columbia,* an America's Cup winner in 1899 and 1901.

5. When the Beatles performed at the Forest Hills Stadium in 1964, they arrived at the venue in a helicopter.

ALONG THE WAY

● 67 Av

● 63 Dr-Rego Park

Knish Nosh. The softball-sized knishes here are made much the same as they were when the restaurant opened in 1952.

Ben's Best Kosher Deli. For more than 60 years, Ben's has served matzo ball soup, chopped liver, and other deli classics.

Elmhurst Av

Jackson Hts-Roosevelt Av

Steinway St

Chao Thai. Spice fanatics will find plenty to love at this Thai hole-in-the-wall, where "hot" is the default setting.

Himalayan Yak. Nepalese and Tibetan cuisine is on offer here— don't forget to try the butter tea.

The Astor Room. This speakeasy-style bar, with cocktails named for actors, is located in a former film-studio cafeteria.

N

Grand Central Pkwy

Homelawn St

Edgerton Blvd

Kingston Pl

Wexford Terrace

164th St

Captain Tilly Park

169 St
F

88th Ave

173rd St

175th St

1 min

162nd St

Highland Ave

170th St

168th St

5 min

Parsons Blvd

172nd St

8

Parsons Blvd
E-F

9

89th Ave

164th St

Jamaica Ave

168th Pl

10 mi

7

161st St

Liberty Ave

1

153rd St

Rufus King Park

6

4

2

3

160th St

Merrick Blvd

15 mi

1 min

158th St

Guy R Brewer Blvd

94th Ave

150 th St

South Rd

20 mi

5 min

10 min

F **E** **Jamaica Center-Parsons/Archer**
J **Z** **Jamaica-179 St**

to Jamaica-179 St
to Jamaica Center-Parsons/Archer

Jamaica is one of the first neighborhoods many tourists see when they visit NYC, as they pass through John F. Kennedy International Airport. It's also at the ends of several subway lines: the E, J, and Z all converge on Jamaica Center, while the F terminates nearby.

Jamaica takes its name from the Jameco Native Americans, who lived in the area before Dutch settlers. The area was incorporated in 1814, and when the official consolidation of New York's various cities and towns took place in 1898, Jamaica became the county seat of Queens. To this day, many of the borough's most important buildings—the Supreme Court, Queens Civil Court, and the Queens Public Library's central branch—are located right around the Jamaica Center subway stop.

There's also plenty to see further from the subway stations. Jamaica Avenue, the neighborhood's main shopping drag, is home to a bevy of historic buildings, including King Manor and the Beaux-Arts Jamaica Savings Bank building. Off of Jamaica Avenue, especially near the 179 St stop, the neighborhood turns residential, although Hillside Avenue is another commercial thoroughfare.

To explore all of this, you have your pick of starting points. From the E, J, or Z, you'll be in the thick of Jamaica's business district; take the F to 179 St, and you'll see more of the small, single-family homes that are characteristic of the area. No matter where you start from, though, you're sure to fall for this historic neighborhood's charms.

to Jamaica-179 St
to Jamaica Center-Parsons/Archer

① Rufus King Park. This small park was named for Rufus King, a lawyer, Federalist sympathizer, and framer of the Constitution. He owned the land (and the house that became King Manor) from 1805 until his death in 1827.

② King Manor Museum. Rufus King's home, which sits at the center of the park, was later converted into a museum dedicated to preserving his family's legacy.

③ Jamaica Center for Arts & Learning. Think of this cultural center as a catchall for creative pursuits; at any time, it might host an art exhibit, a West African dance performance, jazz combos, and even more.

④ Grace Church. Although this Episcopalian church was first established in the 17th century, its current landmarked building wasn't erected until 1862. A small cemetery is part of the complex; Rufus King is interred there.

⑤ Major Mark Park. Although this park was named for a solider who died in World War I, the monument at its center is actually dedicated to the military personnel who served in the Union Army during the Civil War.

⑥ Jamaica Market. Located on bustling Jamaica Avenue, this food hall features stands selling all sorts of foods, including West Indian and Chinese cuisine. Other vendors sell books, fragrances, and more.

⑦ City Rib Bar-B-Que. The smoked-meat specialties at this BBQ joint are served with house-made sauces. The Kings is tomato-and-molasses–based, while the Queens is made with mustard, whiskey, chiles, and more.

⑧ Spicy Lanka. In spite of its unassuming storefront, the walls of this Sri Lankan restaurant are covered in colorful murals. The setting is transportive, as is the menu, filled with curries, *biryani*, and *kothu roti*, a Sri Lankan street food.

⑨ Bellitte Bicycles. Established in 1918, this cycling shop has the distinction of being the oldest bicycle store in the country. Stock up on helmets, tools, and other gear, along with commuter- and trail-friendly two-wheelers.

F E
J Z

5 FACTS OFF THE

[F] [E]
[J] [Z]

1. One of the city's oldest cemeteries, Prospect Cemetery, is located near the York College campus; it's closed to the public.

2. King Kullen, a chain that claims to be "America's first supermarket," opened on Jamaica Avenue in 1930.

3. Jamaica has a particularly rich hip-hop history, with artists like 50 Cent, Nicki Minaj, Onyx, and members of G Unit hailing from the area.

4. Rufus King's son, John Alsop King, would later go on to become the 20th governor of New York state.

5. The Jamaica Center stop is one of the newest in the system, having opened in 1988.

ALONG THE WAY

Sutphin Blvd-Archer Av (J)   Briarwood-Van Wyck Blvd (E-F)

Rincon Salvadoreño. Jury duty refugees crowd this Salvadorean spot for its *pupusas* and fried plantains.

Maple Grove Cemetery. This small graveyard has hosted events like jazz concerts and historic reenactments.

75 Av (E-F)   **111 St (J-Z)**   **Woodhaven Blvd (J-Z)**

East Ocean Palace. Grab dumplings and other small plates from steaming carts at this dim-sum restaurant.

Five Points of Observation. Kathleen McCarthy's six-foot-tall sculptures can be found on five stops, beginning with 111 St.

Forest Park. Set over more than 500 acres, this park features a carousel, a bandshell, and other attractions.

N

2

95th Ave

Lefferts Blvd

120th St

123rd St

Atlantic Ave

127th St

130th St

101st Ave

13nd St

97th Ave

9

7

125th St

8

103rd Ave

5

101st Ave

123rd St

Liberty Ave

1

103rd Ave

3

126th St

125th St

127th St

4

118th St

117th St

1 min

Liberty Ave

124th St

107th Ave

103rd Ave

Lefferts Blvd

6

5 min

107th Ave

116th St

109th Ave

118th St

10 min

101st St

15 min

Linden Blvd

A **Ozone Park**
Lefferts Blvd

Van Wyck Exp

to Ozone Park-Lefferts Blvd

Exit the A train at the end of the line and you'll end up on Liberty Avenue, one of the biggest thoroughfares running through the neighborhood of Richmond Hill. (Contrary to the subway stop's name, Ozone Park is actually a ways north.) Liberty is lined with colorful storefronts that reflect the area's diverse population: Guyanese-Chinese restaurants, an Ayurvedic spa, Caribbean bakeries, and shops selling elegant Indian saris.

The area is named for Edward Richmond, a landscape architect who planned the community in the 19th century. Richmond Hill was originally a bedroom community for wealthy Manhattanites, and as the years progressed, the first wave of immigrants—many of them Italian, Irish, and German—came to the area. (One of its storied German restaurants, the Triangle Hofbrau, attracted the likes of Mae West and Babe Ruth, but ultimately closed in 1999.)

In the later part of the 20th century, the area's demographics changed as more immigrants from Latin America, the Caribbean, and South Asia moved to Richmond Hill. Parts of the neighborhood are known as Little Guyana, thanks to the large Indo-Guyanaese community that has settled here; there's also Little Punjab, evident in the sari shops and Sikh temples found around Liberty Avenue and beyond.

The mishmash of cultures makes Richmond Hill one of the city's most fascinating spots to visit. It's a neighborhood where you can by West Indian spices, Punjabi-style pizza, and beef-filled patties within a few blocks of each other—and it's all at the end of the A.

to Ozone Park-Lefferts Blvd

1 **Phagwah Parade.** During the neighborhood's most vibrant celebration every March, residents celebrate the Hindu holiday by throwing colored powders, wearing brightly-colored saris, and playing traditional music.

2 **Tandoori Hut.** As the name implies, this restaurant specializes in tandoori chicken—but not just the type from your local Indian takeout joint. The green-tinted *haryali tikka*, for instance, is rubbed with mint and cilantro.

3 **ShaktiSaree.** Incredibly colorful fabrics and decorations beckon visitors to this Liberty Avenue storefront, which is filled with bright saris (including ones for weddings), jewelry, religious artifacts, and other ephemera.

4 **Dave West Indian Imports.** Guyanese immigrants in Richmond Hill stock up on curry powder, rice, chow mein (Guyanese-Chinese cuisine is a big thing), and other ingredients at this shop.

5 **Singh's Roti Shop and Bar.** A neighborhood staple for more than two decades, this West Indian restaurant serves a wide swath of dishes: curries, chow meins, and appetizers like pepper chicken and traditional doubles.

6 **Little Guyana Bake Shop.** The name of this shop isn't just in reference to the community it's in; the bakery also sells meat patties, plait bread, and rum-soaked black cake, all Guyanese specialties.

7 **Maha Lakshmi Mandir.** The building that houses this Hindu temple is one of the most distinctive in Richmond Hill. It also hosts celebrations every year for Phagwah and Diwali.

8 **Hibiscus Restaurant & Bar.** One of Richmond Hill's many Guyanese restaurants melds West Indian and Chinese styles of cooking in dishes like jerk chicken fried rice or chicken with bora and cabbage.

9 **Sikh Cultural Society of New York.** After a fire destroyed a Sikh gurdwara in 2002, this new center was built, offering services, events, and daily free meals to the community in Richmond Hill.

A

5 FACTS OFF THE A

1. Even though the subway stop is named for Ozone Park, it's actually located in Richmond Hill.
2. Richmond Hill was home to famous New Yorkers like Jacob Riis, former Yankees announcer Bob Sheppard, and the Marx Brothers.
3. There are three separate ends to the A train: the Ozone Park stop, and the Far Rockaway–Mott Ave and Beach 116th Street stops.
4. In Martin Scorsese's *Goodfellas,* Robert De Niro's character was based on real-life Richmond Hill mobster James Burke.
5. Richmond Hill High School first opened in 1899, and since then, it's graduated students like Rodney Dangerfield and Phil Rizzuto.

104 St

Rockaway Blvd

Police Officer Nicholas Demutiis Park. Named for a NYPD officer who died in the area, this small park is notable for its bocce courts.

Esquire Diner. Mobsters once frequented this long-standing diner, which serves burgers, triple-decker sandwiches, and much more.

Mike's Tavern. This neighborhood pub has a devoted crowd of regulars, who come for cold beers and camaraderie.

Bayside Cemetery. This cemetery, founded in the 19th century, is one of NYC's oldest Jewish cemeteries.

Tudor Village. The southern end of Ozone Park is filled with lovely Tudor-style homes, as well as a small park.

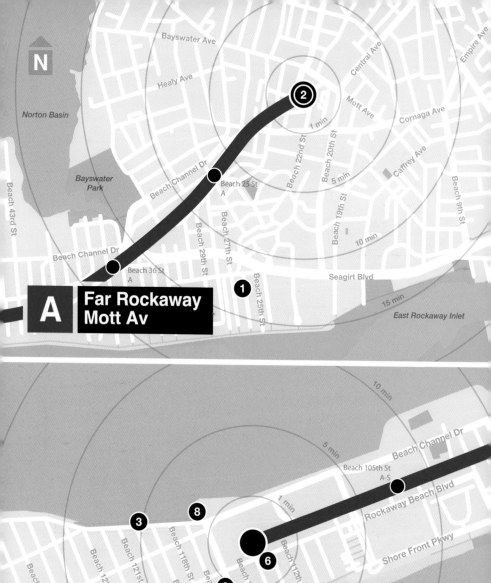

to Far Rockaway-Mott Ave
to Rockaway Park-Beach 116 St

At the end of Queens, you'll find the seaside hideaway known as Rockaway Beach. Well, it's not exactly hidden—the Ramones did name a song for it, after all—but the Rockaways are about 20 miles from Manhattan, and seem a world away from the rest of the city.

Like many of NYC's waterfront areas, the Rockaways became popular in the 19th century, since city folk could go there to cool off in the summer. In 1901, an amusement park, Rockaways' Playland, opened at Beach 98th Street; the famous Far Rockaway bungalows were constructed soon after. But thanks, in part, to Robert Moses—who planned two major thoroughfares there, not to mention housing projects—the landscape of the neighborhood changed as the 20th century progressed.

In recent years, Rockaway Beach has experienced a resurgence; hip businesses like Rockaway Taco and Rippers moved in, and a wave of newcomers joined the crowds who visit the beach every summer. But tragedy struck in 2012, when Hurricane Sandy hit. Much of the boardwalk and beach was swept away, and more than 100 homes in Breezy Point burned to the ground. It's taken a while, but the area is bouncing back: the beach and boardwalk have been repaired, and Breezy Point residents are rebuilding.

The two ends of the A have different vibes: Far Rockaway is more densely packed and city-like, while Beach 116th is more of a seaside community. Both ends are accessible via the bridge that crosses Broad Channel, offering a lovely view of the waterfront.

to Far Rockaway-Mott Ave
to Rockaway Park-Beach 116 St

1 **Far Rockaway Bungalows Historic District.** This area was once home to hundreds of bungalows used as summer rentals; around 90 of those historic homes remain on the blocks around Beach 24th, 25th, and 26th Streets.

2 **Respite.** Artist Jason Rohlf's glass murals were installed as part of a larger rehabilitation of the Far Rockaway-Mott Ave station; the colorful, abstract panels beam rays of bright light into the A terminus.

3 **Beach Channel Park.** On the 116th side of the peninsula, this park faces Jamaica Bay and the Gateway National Recreation Area. It's also home to a 9/11 memorial dedicated to the Rockaway residents who were victims.

4 **Cuisine by Claudette.** Claudette Flatow's cozy spot opened in 2012 and has since become a community gathering spot. Flatow serves healthy eats (smoothies, salads), baked goods, and what might be the area's best coffee.

5 **Rockaway Beach.** Beachcombers of all stripes come to the Rockaways to surf, swim, or simply enjoy the waterfront scenery. Post-Sandy, several new concession and comfort stands have opened to service beach bums.

6 **The Blue Bungalow.** Bring a bit of the Rockaways back with you by visiting this shop, which sells jewelry, home goods, and other tchotchkes inspired by the beach. An adjacent spa offers facials and massages.

7 **Flight 587 Memorial Park.** This memorial was dedicated five years after the 2001 crash of American Airlines Flight 587. Designed by artist Freddy Rodriguez, it lists the names of the dead across granite stones.

8 **The Wharf Bar & Grill.** A staple of the Rockaways for decades (and one that bounced back after Sandy), this waterfront bar is an excellent spot to grab a beer and a basket of peel-and-eat shrimp as you gaze over Jamaica Bay.

9 **Rockaway Beach Surf Shop.** Local surfer Tom Sena opened this store in 1972, and it's been serving the Rockaways' devoted wave riders ever since. Stock up on boards (including stand-up paddleboards), gear, clothing, and more.

A

5 FACTS OFF THE A

1. One of the oldest newspapers in the Rockaways, *The Wave*, debuted in 1893 and still publishes to this day.

2. At about 14 miles long, Rockaway Beach is among the largest urban beachs in the United States.

3. Until 1955, the Far Rockaway station was part of the Long Island Rail Road, not the MTA.

4. The H shuttle train returned after nearly 20 years away in the wake of Hurricane Sandy.

5. In the Rockaways' heyday, celebrities like Mae West, Mary Pickford, and W.C. Fields stayed there.

Beach 98 St

Beach 90 St

Rockaway Taco. The fish tacos, fresh guacamole, and fried plantains are all worth the wait at this hip taco shack.

Bungalow Bar & Restaurant. This pub features a drink called the Rockaway Resilience, in honor of the post-Sandy recovery.

| Beach 60 St | Beach 36 St | Broad Channel |

Marina 59. Boats dock at this small marina, which once housed a boat hotel (called, fittingly, the Boatel).

Symphonic Convergence 1&2. Hundreds of overlapping faces on this glass mosaic symbolize the spirit of the community.

Jamaica Bay Wildlife Refuge. The area around Jamaica Bay is an excellent birding spot, and rangers here lead tours.

to Euclid Av

Like the end of the 3 at New Lots Ave, the C train terminates in East New York. It's a local stop on an express line—a fairly sleepy station in comparison to many others along the IND line. The Euclid Ave stop is close to what was once commonly called City Line, near Cypress Hills and the dividing line between Brooklyn and Queens.

Also like the end of the 3, the neighborhood surrounding the subway stop has been known as an underserved area, though that may be changing. This end of East New York has some reminders of its historic past: both Pitkin Avenue and the rail yard, where C and A trains are stored and maintained, are named for John R. Pitkin, the Connecticut tradesman who originally developed the land in the 19th century. But the poverty and discriminatory housing practices that have plagued many New York neighborhoods have been an issue here.

In recent years, chatter about gentrification coming to East New York has started—and indeed, Mayor Bill de Blasio is using the neighborhood as an example of his new affordable-housing plans. But it remains to be seen whether this largely residential section will change too much. Many of the side streets are lined with brick row homes, some with unique and colorful facades; you'll see flags from different countries, including Trinidad and Puerto Rico, being flown during the day. The main thoroughfares—Liberty Avenue and Pitkin Avenue—aren't quite as bustling as other Brooklyn arteries, but are central areas for the community nevertheless.

to Euclid Av

1 **Little Trini Spot.** Opened by longtime neighborhood resident and restaurateur Cynthia Hosein, this Trinidadian storefront sells dishes like oxtail roti, fish cakes, and chicken curry. Top your selection with one of the hot sauces on offer, which Hosein makes using her own homegrown hot peppers.

2 **City Line Park.** The former Ridgewood Pumping Station was turned into a small park in the mid-20th century, and a 2007 facelift added more green space and recreational areas to the park. Its name comes from the fact that the line separating Brooklyn from Queens was once close by.

3 **Napoli's Pizza.** For a quick bite in the area, try this corner pizzeria, a neighborhood staple for more than 40 years. The shop offers the usual suspects—cheese pies, Sicilian slices, calzones—along with a few neighborhood-appropriate surprises, like Jamaican beef patties.

4 **Upon This Rock Community Garden.** Founded approximately 30 years ago, this 4,000-square-foot green space is filled with plant life, including vegetables, flowers, and different varieties of trees. There are also several composting bins for the neighborhood's ecologically-minded residents.

5 **Conduit Blvd Median Strip.** Conduit Boulevard (which becomes Conduit Avenue in Queens) has a large, grassy strip in the middle, some parts of which seem almost park-like.

6 **Cypress Hills Library.** Although a branch of this library has existed since 1955, the current red-brick building dates to 1995. Its modern structure, with plenty of natural light from an interior skylight, is notable for its dynamic entrance, with a brightly colored piece by Rolando Briseno.

7 **El Rey II.** Domincan specialties dominate the menu at this local spot, with different *cuchifritos* (including pork skin and fried potatoes), *mofongos*, and chicken-and-rice dishes. There's also a selection of fresh-squeezed juices (carrot, passion fruit) available.

C

1. Euclid Ave connects to the express A along the IND line, and is the last express stop on the line in this part of the city.

2. Construction on Euclid Ave began before World War II, but was halted as an austerity measure. It finally opened in 1948.

3. Because of that, the design of the station is different from most other C train stations—but the differences, like tile size, are slight.

4. The Charles Bronson movie *Death Wish 3* was filmed, in part, in East New York (a sign for Fountain Avenue appears in the trailer).

5. The subway stop deposits riders onto Pitkin Ave, named for the merchant who initially developed the neighborhood.

ALONG THE WAY

● Van Siclen Av   ● Broadway Junction

Festac Grill. Be prepared for fiery dishes and exotic meats (tripe, goat offal) at this Nigerian restaurant.

Brooklyn, New Morning. The late Al Loving's spectacular gass mural consists of 75 glass panels in hues as varied as the rainbow.

Ralph Av

Utica Av

Nostrand Av

Central Brooklyn Jazz Consortium. This musical organization runs the Central Brooklyn Jazz Festival and the Brooklyn Jazz Hall of Fame.

Peaches. Southern home cooking—in the form of catfish and grits, fried flounder, and ribs—is on the menu at this Bed-Stuy hotspot.

Nostrand Avenue Pub. In warmer weather, people sip pints of domestic and craft beer in the backyard of this low-key bar.

N

Sutter Ave

Montauk Ave

Warwick St

Schenck Ave

Barbey St

Jerome St

Hendrix St

Cleveland St

Ashford St

Dumont Ave

Van Siclen Ave

New Lots Ave

Linwood St

Hegeman Ave

⑥

④

⑤

Elton St

② ⑦

Van Siclen Av
2 - 3 - 4 - 5

1 min

①

Ashford St

Warwick St

Riverdale Ave

Hendrix St

Schenck Ave

Barbey St

Jerome St

New Lots Ave

Linden Blvd

5 min

Cleveland St

Hegeman Ave

10 min

Cozine Ave

③

Linden Park

Van Siclen Ave

Schenck St

Vermont St

Linden Blvd

15 min

Flatlands Ave

3 **New Lots Av**

to New Lots Av

Like many areas at the end of the line, the 3 train terminates in a part of town that's more residential and slightly sleepier than the city's center. East New York is also one of the city's poorer areas, and is perhaps better known for high crime rates than anything else. But that viewpoint ignores much of the change that has been happening in the area in the last decade.

Historically, East New York has included smaller areas like City Line, Cypress Hills, and New Lots, which gives the subway stop at the end of the 3 its name. The area was settled by the Dutch in the 17th century, and built up by John Pitkin in the 19th century. Although the neighborhood has always been working-class, its demographic makeup changed in the 20th century, with more African Americans and Hispanic residents moving in. Not long after, discriminatory practices—including blockbusting and redlining, not to mention white flight—contributed to the neighborhood's decline, from which it's still recovering.

That recovery has largely been led by neighborhood residents, who have worked tirelessly over the years to create a more harmonious community. From the end of the 3, you're able to see some of the fruits of that labor. Witness the East New York Farmers' Market, a haven for fresh, seasonal goods, or the plethora of gardens in the area. At Arts East New York, local artists can showcase their work or participate in events intended to bolster neighborhood pride. They're welcome additions to an area that, while historically underserved, is taking steps toward change.

to New Lots Av

1 **New Lots Community Church.** This small, wood-frame church, which was built by Dutch settlers in 1824, looks like it belongs in a small New England town rather than Brooklyn. There are two cemeteries, one of which has graves dating back to the 18th century.

2 **Arts East New York.** This organization doesn't focus solely on art projects, although it does host exhibitions at its Hegeman Street studio. It also functions as a community center, planning projects and events intended to bolster East New York. Past events have included yoga classes, film screenings, a holiday tree lighting, and a paint-and-sip class (including free wine).

3 **Linden Park.** Athletic types will find plenty to do at this park, which has a track, basketball courts, and tennis courts. It's named for Linden Boulevard, the large thoroughfare that abuts the space (and gets its name, in turn, for the abundance of linden trees that line the way).

4 **East New York Farmers' Market.** This seasonal market features more than a dozen vendors; it's an excellent place to get hard-to-find produce like callaloo and Scotch bonnet peppers. It's run by East New York Farms, which has been providing the neighborhood with fresh produce since 1998.

5 **New Lots Pedestrian Plaza.** Small though it may be, this triangle of car-free space, at the point where New Lots and Livonia Avenues meet, is beloved by locals for creating an open area where residents can congregate. Tables and chairs allow denizens to sit outdoors when the weather is nice, provided you don't mind the sound of the subway overhead.

6 **New Visions Garden.** For more than 20 years, neighborhood residents have tended to this small patch of greenery. It also has a system for collecting and reusing rainwater.

7 **Livonia Yard.** Fun fact: 3 trains aren't the only subways that get serviced at this rail yard; it's also the maintenance yard for the trains used on the 42nd Street Shuttle.

3

5 FACTS OFF THE 3

1. Until 1983, the 3 ended at the Flatbush Ave-Brooklyn College stop, while the 2 ended in East New York.
2. Legendary musicians George and Ira Gershwin were born in a house on Snediker Avenue.
3. The area was named New Lots in the 17th century, to contrast with the neighborhood Old Lots, which was closer to what is now Flatbush.
4. A plaque near Livonia Avenue commemorates the New Lots African Burial Ground, where remains of enslaved Africans were found.
5. This isn't the only New Lots Avenue subway stop; another stop along the L shares the exact same name.

3

If you plan to exit the 3 at this station, don't plan on exiting onto Junius Street: there's no entrance on that particular block.

Betsy Head Park. This 10-acre park has a pool, built as part of the Works Progress Administration, and has hosted live music.

Kingston Av   **Nostrand Av**   **Grand Army Plaza**

Sweet Expressions. Indulge your sweet tooth with Kosher gelato, candy, and other sugary desserts.

Catfish. Inspired by New Orleans cuisine, this restaurant serves jambalaya, gumbo, po' boys, and other Cajun specialties.

Franny's. The pizza at this venerated restaurant is wood-fired, made with locally-sourced ingredients, and totally delicious.

to Canarsie-Rockaway Pkwy

At the end of Brooklyn, the sleepy neighborhood of Canarsie beckons. The terminus of the L is a true end of line, with the Canarsie rail yard situated nearby. But many of the neighborhood's attractions, including a waterfront park and pier that are beloved by locals, are a hike from the subway—one that's worth taking.

In the 17th century, present-day Canarsie was part of Flatlands, one of the five towns in the Dutch settlement known as Breukelen. A bit of that history remains, not too far from the end of the L. One of the city's oldest structures, the home of Dutch settler Pieter Claesen Wyckoff, was built in 1652, and what remains is now a museum.

Canarsie's waterfront locale led to the ascent of two different industries: fishing and tourism. Jamaica Bay was an asset for the area's fisherman, who supplied seafood to the rest of New York City. Out-of-towners flocked to Canarsie's beaches, and in 1907, Golden City Amusement Park opened. That success was be short-lived: Pollution in Jamaica Bay all but killed the fishing industry, and the Great Depression hurt the resorts. Much later, Canarsie would be further devastated by Hurricane Sandy, which damaged many area homes.

Today, Canarsie is a diverse hamlet that has a suburban feel—largely due to the fact that much of the neighborhood is most easily accessed by car. Main thoroughfares like Rockaway Parkway and Flatlands Avenue are dense with shops and people, but the closer you get to Jamaica Bay, the more open the area feels.

to Canarsie-Rockaway Pkwy

1 **Canarsie Park.** Bordered by Seaview Avenue and the bay, this park is especially popular for picnicking families, cricket teams (who play on the weekends), and skateboarders drawn to a skate park that opened in 2012.

2 **Canarsie Pier.** Part of the Gateway National Recreation Area, this pier extends 600 feet out onto Jamaica Bay, providing excellent views of the surrounding wildlife. It's a popular spot for amateur fishers.

3 **Brooklyn Plantology by Lapide.** Located within Brooklyn Terminal Market, this family-run shop sells all manner of flora, from flowers to cacti, and also hosts events like wine-tasting sessions and a seasonal pumpkin patch.

4 **Wyckoff House Museum.** To see what life was like in 17th-century Breukelen, visit Pieter Wyckoff's home, one of the oldest buildings in New York City. It's a hike from the L, but history buffs will appreciate the tours.

5 **Canarsie History Museum.** Neighborhood native Ramon Martinez is behind this organization that documents the area's past. It puts on the annual Canarsie History Fair, which happens every summer.

6 **Sebago Canoe Club.** Members of this volunteer-run organization set sail from Paerdegat Basin, a small inlet connected to Jamaica Bay. The group leads open paddles, kayaking tours, and clinics for kids.

7 **Bamboo Garden.** In a nod to the area's diverse population, this restaurant serves Asian-Caribbean fusion, with dishes like jerk pork fried rice and stewed oxtail. It also hosts popular weekly karaoke nights.

8 **Armando's.** You can't get much more convenient than this pizzeria, located right next to the end of the L. Open since 1960, the restaurant serves piping-hot plain and Sicilian slices underneath photos of mid-century Canarsie.

9 **La Baguette Shop.** Canarsie is home to one of NYC's biggest Haitian enclaves, and this bakery provides a link to that culture, selling Caribbean patties in flavors like beef and codfish, pastries, and the popular Haitian soda Cola Lacaye.

L

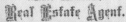

5
FACTS
OFF THE

L

1. Famous former Canarsie residents include Starbucks CEO Howard Schultz and popular broadcaster Al Roker.

2. You might want to bring earplugs to Canarsie Pier: Its proximity to JFK Airport means low-flying planes frequently roar over the water.

3. The *Canarsie Courier* has been covering neighborhood news since 1921 and is Brooklyn's oldest weekly newspaper.

4. Yes, there's an odd little log cabin on Flatlands Avenue; it was once an ice-cream parlor, and is now a real-estate office.

5. Canarsie's name is likely derived from the name of a group of Lenape Native Americans that originally settled the area.

Broadway Junction   Bushwick Av-Aberdeen St

The Evergreens Cemetery.
This graveyard, which borders
both Queens and Brooklyn,
has a memorial to the Triangle
Shirtwaist fire victims.

The subway stop here is the
attraction: It's the only station
whose entrance is within a car
dealership.

DeKalb Av

Morgan Av

Montrose Av

Maria Hernandez Park. Named for a slain community activist, this small park has a dog park and a farmer's market.

Roberta's. This popular pizza spot lives up to the hype, serving delicious, inventive pies in a hip, rustic space.

Dun-Well Doughnuts. Find vegan versions of doughy confections—including jelly-filled and glazed varieties—at this Bushwick bakeshop.

Kingston-
Throop Avs
C

N

15 min

Utica Av
A-C

Atlantic Ave

10 min

Pacific St

Kingston Ave

Bergen St

Bergen St

St Marks Ave

St. Johns
Park

St Marks Ave

2

3

Prospect Pl

5 min

Prospect Pl

Brower Park

1

Park Pl

Sterling Pl

Rochester Ave

1 min

8 Kingston Av
2-3-4-5

Lincoln Pl

9

Kingston Ave

4

Eastern Pkwy

7

Union St

5

6

Albany Ave

Troy Ave

Schenectady Ave

Utica Ave

Lincoln
Terrace Park

Empire Blvd

E New York Ave

Lefferts Ave

Remsen Ave

Rutland Rd

4 **Crown Hts
Utica Av**

to Crown Hts-Utica Av

Crown Heights is a neighborhood in flux. While the western edge, especially around Franklin Avenue, is experiencing rapid changes, the corner close to the edge of the 4 hasn't seen as huge a shift. Businesses that would normally be the harbingers of gentrification have arrived—an upscale pizza joint, a fitness center—but this end of Crown Heights has yet to transform fully.

The neighborhood was, at one point, an enclave for the very wealthy—a section of St. Marks Avenue was even referred to as "Millionaire's Row," thanks to the proliferation of mansions on the block. In the 20th century, Crown Heights became home to several diverse populations: groups of West Indian immigrants moved to the area, as did African Americans as part of the "Great Migration" from the southern United States. At the same time, a large Jewish community—in particular, a large Hasidic community—established itself in Crown Heights.

At times, tensions between area residents have boiled over, most notably in the case of the 1991 Crown Heights Riots, which happened after a neighborhood child was killed in a car accident. In the aftermath of the three-day riots, leaders from the area's black and Jewish communities, as well as residents, sought ways to bring the differing groups together.

Those efforts were largely successful, and now, there are restaurants, shops, and cultural centers serving the area's residents—including a slew of newcomers, attracted by Crown Heights' diversity and low rents.

to Crown Hts-Utica Av

1 **Weeksville Heritage Center.** In the 19th century, this area was home to one of the country's first free black communities. Now, the historic homes of Weeksville are open to the public for tours and events.

2 **Brooklyn Children's Museum.** The country's first child-focused museum originally opened in Crown Heights in 1899. It's since become a community hub, and hosts readings, art programs, and interactive exhibits.

3 **Brower Park.** Named for a former City Parks commissioner, this park—the original site of the Brooklyn Children's Museum—has a skate park and plenty of green space; it's also popular with the neighborhood's dog-lovers.

4 ***Good Morning and Good Night***. Hugo Consuegra's art can be found throughout the Crown Heights-Utica Ave subway stop, with bright suns and moons adorning the subway walls, gates, and other spots.

5 **Lincoln Terrace Park.** The biggest draw at this 17-acre park is its cluster of tennis courts, which were renovated in 2014 and host both adults and kids. Its tree-lined pathways are especially pretty on spring days.

6 **Conrad's Bakery.** Owner Conrad Ifill has been baking Trinidadian treats at this local favorite for more than 30 years. Ifill's fresh-baked loaves of hard dough bread, a Caribbean delicacy, are legendary.

7 **Alumni.** Once home to the famed sneaker shop Rugged Sole, this store still sells cool kicks by Stussy, Nike, and Puma, along with other streetwear brands, in a sleek, refurbished storefront.

8 **Basil Pizza & Wine Bar.** In keeping with Crown Heights' Jewish history, this intimate restaurant serves an entirely kosher menu, from the wood-fired pizzas to the reasonably-priced wine list.

9 **Jewish Children's Museum.** Located in a modern, award-winning building, this ten-year-old institution hosts interactive exhibits that school kids on the history of Judaism, life as a Jewish person, and more.

4

5 FACTS OFF THE 4

1. Despite its name, there's no entrance or exit at Utica Avenue for this particular subway stop.
2. Famous Crown Heights residents include record executive Clive Davis, Norman Mailer, and Congresswoman Shirley Chisholm.
3. At one point, the population of the community of Weeksville exceeded 500 people; it was all but gone by the 20th century.
4. Before it was called Crown Heights, the neighborhood was referred to as "Crow Hill."
5. Eastern Parkway, the main east-west route, was designed by Central Park architects Frederick Law Olmsted and Calvert Vaux.

ALONG THE WAY

● Franklin Av

● Atlantic Av–Barclays Ctr

4

Barboncino. In just a few years, this Neapolitan-style pizzeria has become one of NYC's most acclaimed.

Williamsburgh Savings Bank Tower. This historic structure, built in the 1920s, was once Brooklyn's tallest building.

Nevins St   **Borough Hall**   **Bowling Green**

BRIC House. This onetime historic theatre is a hub for local musicians, theater troupes, and other performing artists.

Cadman Plaza. At the foot of the Brooklyn Bridge you'll find this small park, home to a World War II memorial.

Castle Clinton. Once an immigration station and tourist attraction, this fort now hosts tours, concerts, and more.

N

Avenue D

Newkirk Ave

Newkirk Av
2-5

Foster Ave

Bedford Ave

Rogers Ave

Flatbush Ave

Farragut Rd

Farragut Rd

E 29th St

E 31st St

New York Ave

Glenwood Rd

9

E 26th St

3

Glenwood Rd

E 23rd St

4

Campus Rd

5

Avenue H

Brooklyn Ave

1

Brooklyn College

2

1 min

Nostrand Ave

Flatbush Ave

7

Bedford Ave

E 31st St

Avenue I

6

E 32nd St

5 min

Avenue I

8

Avenue J

10 min

New York Ave

15 min

2 5 **Flatbush Av**
Brooklyn College

to Flatbush Av-Brooklyn College

If you want to fit in as a local when you get off the 2 or 5 train at Brooklyn College, call the neighborhood "the Junction." Though the nickname refers to the point where Flatbush and Nostrand Avenues meet, it also makes sense for other reasons. The subway stop is located at the intersection of several neighborhoods: Midwood, Flatbush, and Ditmas Park.

When the Dutch settlement of Breuckelen was created in the 17th century, Flatbush was one of the first six towns, although it was known as *Midwout* (later, Midwood). The area was largely rural farmland until the late 19th century, when the different boroughs were consolidated; that, plus the arrival of an early rail system in the area, led to Flatbush becoming more of an exurb for wealthy New Yorkers. (Vestiges of this can be found in "Victorian Flatbush," sections of the neighborhood where gorgeous 19th-century homes remain.)

As the 20th century progressed, harbingers of change arrived. The Vitagraph Studio opened in 1906, producing silent films and later, TV shows, in Midwood. (A smokestack at Avenue M and 14th Street is all that remains from the complex.) Brooklyn College opened in 1930, bringing students and academic types to the area. And in the later part of the 20th century, the neighborhood's ethnic makeup changed again, with many immigrants from the Caribbean and South Asia settling in the area.

Nowadays, the Junction is a melting pot where cultures, neighborhoods, and people meet. Take the 2 or 5 to the end point to experience this fusion for yourself.

to Flatbush Av-Brooklyn College

① Brooklyn College. Part of the City University of New York system, this college has attracted noteworthy faculty members, including Allen Ginsberg (who taught there in the '80s and '90s) and Jack Gelber.

② Brooklyn Center for the Performing Arts. The main Walt Whitman Theatre, which opened in 1955, hosts performers of all sorts, including dance troupes, children's music acts, and pop groups.

③ Exquisite Supreme. There are plenty of jerk chicken spots near Flatbush Avenue, but this no-frills restaurant offers a mound of spicy, moist chicken that beats the competition. Try the Jamaican-style oxtail, too.

④ Lords Bakery. For more than 40 years, this small bake shop has been serving cookies, pastries, and other treats to hungry Flatbush denizens. It's also known for creating über-realistic photo cakes.

⑤ Doowop Griddle. This small storefront is known for its waffles, served sweet with Nutella or various fruits, or savory (well, savory-ish) with pieces of juicy fried chicken and maple gravy.

⑥ Zelda's Art World. Stock up on all the paints, portrait frames, and sketching materials you'd need at this art-supply store, which also offers classes (cartooning, oil painting, etc.) for artists of all ages.

⑦ Bulletproof Comics. This shop doesn't simply serve comics fans; with skate decks, action figures, and gaming cards (e.g. Magic the Gathering) among the offerings, it's a one-stop shop for geeky pursuits.

⑧ Joost Van Nuyse House. Also called the Coe House, this small cottage was designated a National Historic Landmark more than 40 years ago. The 18th-century home is hidden in plain sight along 34th Street.

⑨ Ashoka Grill. The extensive menu at this Indian restaurant (which uses only halal meat) offers superlative versions of classic dishes, including tandoori chicken, saag paneer, and various biryanis.

2 **5**

1. Although the subway stop was revamped in the 1990s, some of its original 1920 tile work spelling out the name of the station remains.

2. Brooklyn College saw protests during the Vietnam War, as well as performances by anti-war activists like Pete Seeger and Phil Ochs.

3. The area now called Flatbush was originally known as *Midwout* by the Dutch settlers who moved there in the 17th century.

4. Allegedly, Mel Blanc, the original voice of Bugs Bunny, based the iconic cartoon rabbit's accent on the classic Flatbush patois.

5. A group of wild Monk parakeets has lived on the campus of Brooklyn College for decades.

ALONG THE WAY

● Newkirk Av

● Beverly Rd

2 **5**

Taste the Tropics. A neighborhood staple for decades, this ice-cream shop offers unique flavors like coconut and rum raisin.

Kings Theatre. This historic, opulent theater was recently renovated to its former gilded glory.

Erasmus Hall High School. The alumni of this famous school include Barbra Streisand, Neil Diamond, and Mae West.

Wingate Park. Named for the founder of the NRA (yes, really), this park has popular handball and basketball courts.

Culpepper's. This spot specializes in Barbadian cuisine; try the *cou-cou*, a savory mixture of cornmeal and okra topped with fish.

to Franklin Av / Prospect Park

For such a small subway line, the Franklin Avenue Shuttle has an eventful history. It opened in the late 19th century, became the site of one of the deadliest subway accidents, and by the 1980s, it was so disused that it was called a "ghost train." Times have changed, and the small train is now more popular than ever.

Back to that accident: in 1918, a train crashed in the tunnel approaching the Prospect Park stop, killing at least 93 people. The collision, known as the Malbone Street Wreck, was bad enough that Malbone Street itself, which was close to where the crash occurred, was renamed Empire Boulevard.

But the accident didn't contribute to the line's downfall; economics and neglect led to threats of shutting the line down, and one station did close in 1995. But activists in Bedford-Stuyvesant and Crown Heights never gave up on it, and in 1999, the MTA completed a renovation of the shuttle's four remaining stops. Now, more than a decade later, the shuttle serves a rapidly gentrifying area; it's unlikely that it will fall into such disrepair again.

At a little more than a mile long, a trip on the Franklin Avenue Shuttle takes no time at all—seven minutes, thereabouts. Its northern terminus, Franklin Avenue, is on the edge of Bed-Stuy, while the southern end lets riders off in Prospect-Lefferts Gardens. And considering how many lines it connects to—the 2, 3, 4, 5, B, Q, and C—it makes for a convenient, and lively, day trip.

to Franklin Av / Prospect Park

① **Brooklyn Botanic Garden.** There are few better places to unwind than this 52-acre urban oasis, densely packed with native plants and gorgeous flowers of all sorts. Come in the spring, when cherry blossoms flourish.

② **Prospect Park Zoo.** You'll find lions, tigers, and bears—and much more—at this zoo, which opened in 1935 and was renovated in the 1980s. Families come to see its red pandas, Hamadryas baboons, and sea lions.

③ **LeFrak Center at Lakeside.** The former Prospect Park ice-skating rink was re-imagined in 2013 as a picturesque facility where visitors can skate (both roller and ice), as well as play hockey, roller derby, and even curling.

④ **Berg'n.** The team behind the Brooklyn Flea opened this food hall. There are eats from vendors like Ramen Burger and finger-licking Mighty Quinn's BBQ, which you can wash down with one of many craft beers on tap.

⑤ **West Indian-American Day Carnival.** Arguably the city's most colorful festival, this annual fair brings West Indian vendors, food, and musicians to Eastern Parkway. Look for the over-the-top costumes worn by revelers.

⑥ **Ali's Trinidad Roti Shop.** This Bed-Stuy mainstay has been serving Trinidadian specialties for decades. Newbies should try the tasty doubles, a snack of spiced chickpeas sandwiched between two pieces of *bara*.

⑦ **Lincoln Park Tavern.** This hybrid bar-restaurant offers a Mexican-inflected menu on the restaurant side, and a low-key bar serving beer, well drinks, and more on the other side.

⑧ **Peace & Riot.** This shop only opened in 2013, but it already has Bed-Stuy bona fides: Its owners, a local husband-and-wife team, stock a selection of home goods, including African weaved baskets and handmade pillows.

⑨ **Joloff.** A neighborhood staple for 20 years, this spot serves Senegalese dishes beloved by its owner, Papa Diagne. Order *thiéboudienne,* the national dish of Senegal, with fish, vegetables, and the eatery's namesake rice.

S

1. The shuttle originally opened in 1878, making it older than many of the subway lines it now connects to.

2. Ebbets Field, home to the Brooklyn Dodgers, stood a few blocks from the Prospect Park stop; now, it's an apartment complex.

3. Until 1995, the Shuttle had a fifth stop: Dean Street, between the Franklin Avenue and Park Place stations; It closed due to neglect.

4. The late, great comedian Joan Rivers lived at 135 Eastern Parkway, not far from the shuttle, as a child.

5. The Park Place stop is the New York subway system's only one-track station.

ALONG THE WAY

● Botanic Garden   ● Botanic Garden

Brooklyn Museum. This stately museum houses collections of Egyptian artifacts, feminist art, and more.

Franklin Park. In warm weather, the charming patio here is packed with people drinking craft beer.

Botanic Garden

Park Pl

Park Pl

Glady's. Inspired by the area's Caribbean roots, this spot serves dishes like jerk chicken, curries, and plantains.

Gueros. Visit this taqueria on the weekends for its chorizo-spiked breakfast taco, along with the addictive queso.

Hullabaloo Books. The neighborhood's only bookstore hosts literary events and book groups, along with selling tomes.

G Church Av

to Church Av

The end of the G line at Church Ave hasn't actually been a subway terminus for that long. Until 2012, the end of the line was the Smith Ave–9th Street station in Gowanus, with the extension into Kensington being a temporary fix to accommodate track work along the F and G. But residents and businesses in Kensington, Windsor Terrace, and points north championed the extension, which the MTA eventually made permanent.

Having another lifeline into the neighborhood besides the F has been a boon for this sleepy Brooklyn community. Despite its proximity to Manhattan— only about 40 minutes or so on the F line, or a quick transfer on the G— Kensington has yet to become an über-hip neighborhood in the way that Park Slope or Fort Greene have. It's remained relatively affordable and diverse, with immigrants from more than a dozen countries represented.

That variety is most obvious along Church Avenue, one of the neighborhood's main thoroughfares, where you'll find Mexican, Bangladeshi, Japanese, and Polish establishments, among other businesses. If you wander off the main drag, though, you'll see evidence of Kensington's past: side streets, including Albemarle Road, are lined with beautiful old Victorian houses.

Whether you come to Kensington to visit its nearby landmarks—Green-Wood Cemetery, or Prospect Park, which is a short walk from the subway—or simply to soak up its culture, you're sure to be captivated. Its distinctive mix of urban diversity and bucolic charm is unlike many other neighborhoods in the city, and well worth a visit.

to Church Av

1 **Green-Wood Cemetery.** Famous New Yorkers like DeWitt Clinton and Leonard Bernstein are buried here, but Green-Wood is also known for inspiring Central Park designers Frederick Law Olmsted and Calvert Vaux.

2 **Brooklyn Banya.** At these Russian-style baths, you can move from super-hot steam rooms (that can go above 100 degrees) to icy baths to get your blood flowing. There's a small roof deck and Russian food on offer.

3 **Steeplechase Coffee.** This small, homey coffee shop opened in 2011, and is an excellent spot to grab a cup and linger for a bit. The coffee comes from Kings County's own Brooklyn Roasting Company.

4 **Church Cafe & Wine Bar.** Opened in 2014 by a local couple, this snug bar features a solid assortment of wines by the glass, along with Mexican-inspired small plates like *queso fundido* and *poblanos rellenos*.

5 **Sugandha Restaurant.** Kensington's Bengali community has grown exponentially in recent years, and many community members can be found at this restaurant, where you select Bangladeshi specialties from steam tables.

6 **Buzz-a-Rama.** If you're not familiar with slot-car racing, then come to Buzz-a-Rama to get acquainted. Opened by Frank "Buzz" Perri in 1965, the shop is a haven for kids and slot enthusiasts.

7 **Am Thai Bistro.** This family-run restaurant turns out delicious, traditional Thai dishes like *tom kha gai* (coconut milk soup), pad thai, and spicy Panang curry.

8 **Hamilton's.** This corner pub has just about everything you might want from a neighborhood bar: a rotating beer list, good food, good happy-hour specials, and a welcoming, relaxed vibe.

9 **David Shannon Nursery & Florist.** This family-run florist gets especially festive around the holidays: snag pumpkins in autumn, or go around the holidays to get a Christmas tree. (Other plants are also available year-round.)

G

1. One of the more oddly-named streets in Kensington is Old New Utrecht Road, a two-block stretch off of 36th Street.

2. Green-Wood Cemetery was once one of New York's most popular attractions, right behind Niagara Falls in annual visitors.

3. Kensington was originally called Greenfield, but sometime in the 19th century, it was named after the neighborhood in London.

4. Though the G line ends here, the F continues on to Coney Island—but this is its last underground stop.

5. Smell something a little funky in the area? It's probably the Kensington Stables, located at the southwest corner of Prospect Park.

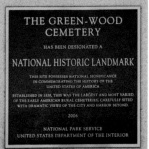

ALONG THE WAY

Fort Hamilton Pkwy · 15th St-Prospect Park

Brooklyn Commune. This cafe also has a strong local connection, with CSA pick-ups and events offered regularly.

The Double Windsor. Wash down gooey mac & cheese with one of 14 carefully selected craft beers including New York-brewed options.

| 7 Av | 4th Av-9 St | Smith-9 Sts |

Prospect Park. The jewel in Brooklyn's crown, this gorgeous park is filled with rolling lawns and plenty of activities.

Four & Twenty Blackbirds. Sisters Emily and Melissa Elsen serve delicious pies (try the salty honey) at this cozy shop.

The Bell House. Comedy shows, live music, and lectures are just some of the events held at this hip former warehouse.

R | **Bay Ridge**
95 St

R

to Bay Ridge-95 St

Bay Ridge is often referred to as a hidden gem within Brooklyn, and after one visit to the neighborhood, it's easy to see why. Bay Ridge hasn't succumbed to the wave of gentrification that hit other Brooklyn areas like Carroll Gardens or Park Slope; instead, it's remained a middle-class enclave, one that's as desirable to live in as it is to visit.

The neighborhood's proximity to the waterfront has long been a draw. Dutch settlers came to the area in the 17th century, and it later became a haven for wealthy businessmen, who built mansions overlooking the harbor. But it wasn't until the R train arrived in 1915 that the real residential expansion of Bay Ridge began: European immigrants (from Italy, Ireland, and Norway) arrived in droves—the population doubled between 1910 and 1924—turning the once-exclusive community into a real neighborhood.

Bay Ridge is also home to some of the city's most impressive civic endeavors. Fort Hamilton, an active military base (the only one in NYC), opened in 1831 and was used as a stronghold during the Civil War. More than a century later, Robert Moses oversaw the development and construction of the Verrazano-Narrows Bridge, which connects Brooklyn to Staten Island. (Bay Ridge residents, 8,000 of whom were uprooted to build the structure, also protested it at the time.)

The Bay Ridge of today has retained its small-town feel, while becoming more diverse; there are thriving Arab-American and Asian communities that have brought restaurants, shops, and culture to the area. From the end of the line, you can easily access both the waterfront, and the main thoroughfares of Third and Fifth Avenues.

to Bay Ridge-95th St

1 **Paneantico Bakery Cafe.** Italian specialties abound at this corner deli and bakery, including dozens of sandwiches, gelato, and baked goods. Whatever you order, be sure to add a sweet, creamy cannoli for dessert.

2 **John Paul Jones Park.** This park, named for the so-called "father of the Navy," overlooks the lengthy span of the Verrazano. Its most notable landmark is a giant Parrott cannon, dedicated as a Civil War memorial.

3 **Shore Road Park.** There's plenty to do at this waterfront park—running, tennis and basketball courts, and more—but the postcard-worthy views of the Statue of Liberty and Staten Island are worth a visit on their own.

4 **Kitty Kiernans.** Opened by an Irish expat in 1996, this bar has a handsome, dark-wood interior, a cadre of friendly regulars, and expertly pulled pints of Guinness (of course).

5 **Harbor Defense Museum.** Located on the grounds of Fort Hamilton, an Army base built in the 19th century, this small museum collects military ephemera, including artifacts from the Revolutionary War and 9/11.

6 **Robicelli's Cupcakes.** Husband-and-wife team and Bay Ridge lifers Matt and Allison Robicelli sell addictive cupcakes (like pumpkin spice and chicken & waffles), along with cakes and pies, from this homey storefront.

7 **Ho Brah Taco Joint.** The owners of this restaurant took inspiration from taquerias across the country for its menu. You can try Cali-inspired burritos and fish tacos, or an *al pastor* riff with slaw, washed down with margaritas.

8 **New York City Marathon.** The route for this 26.2-mile race takes runners through Bay Ridge; after participants cross the Verrazano Bridge, they run along Fourth Avenue, past neighborhood landmarks and cheering spectators.

9 **Nino's Pizza.** Pizza aficionados head to Nino's, a neighborhood institution, for its saucy Grandma slice. Their thin-crust version is heavy on the tomato, and truly worthy cheap eats.

R

5
FACTS
OFF THE

R

1. The classic flick *Saturday Night Fever* was filmed in Bay Ridge, with some spots that show up in the film still around today.

2. The oldest house in Bay Ridge is a beautiful, wooden Greek Revival home, known as the Farrell House; it was built in 1847.

3. With a central span of 4,260 feet, the Verrazano is the longest suspension bridge in the United States.

4. Despite being a Union base, Fort Hamilton was once home to two Confederate fighters: Robert E. Lee and Thomas "Stonewall" Jackson.

5. The southern end of Bay Ridge is occasionally referred to as "Fort Hamilton," a neighborhood within a neighborhood.

JOIN A LEAGUE · SUMMER · S

R

Century 21. This bargain haven opened in Bay Ridge half a century ago, and is less crowded than its Manhattan counterpart.

Leske's Bakery. Hark back to Bay Ridge's Scandinavian past by sampling traditional pastries like kringle and Danish.

Bay Ridge Av   **45 St**   **36 St**

Cedar's Pastry. Try this shop's stretchy mastic ice cream, a delicacy commonly found in Lebanon.

Sunset Park. This park's namesake is clear when you visit at dusk: The sunset from the top of the park is breathtaking.

Melody Lanes. At this old-school bowling alley, the beers and hot dogs are cheap, and leagues frequently take over the lanes.

N

Calvert
Vaux Park

Bay 52nd St

Bay 53rd St

Cropsey Ave

Hart Pl

Coney Island Creek

Stillwell Ave

W 17th St

W 16th St

W 15th St

W 13th St

10 min

5 min

Neptune
F

Neptune Ave

1 min

W 12th St

W 8th St

Neptune Ave

W 21st St

W 20th St

W 19th St

W 17th St

W 16th St

W 15th St

W 23rd St

Mermaid Ave

W 22nd St

Surf Ave

Stillwell Ave

Bowery St

W 8 - NY Aquarium
F-Q

Surf Ave

Lower New York Bay

6

1

5

8

2

7

4

9

3

to Coney Island-Stillwell Av

Since the 19th century, Coney Island has been where New Yorkers go to escape the city's hustle and bustle, all for the cost of a subway fare. Originally a seaside resort (sometimes called "the poor man's Riviera"), the neighborhood quickly became home to three amusement parks: Steeplechase Park, Luna Park, and Dreamland.

Although all three would be gone by the 1960s, the neighborhood remained a destination for vaudeville entertainment and stomach-churning rides. The 150-foot-tall Wonder Wheel, with its panoramic city views, opened in 1920, and the Cyclone roller coaster began operations in 1927. More recently, a new amusement park, also called Luna Park, opened in 2010, bringing glitzy new rides back to the area.

Eventually, more residential buildings came to Coney Island, as did attractions like the New York Aquarium and the Abe Stark ice-skating rink (both thanks to city planner Robert Moses). But the connection to Coney's offbeat past remains strong: Dick Zigun, often called "the mayor of Coney Island," runs Coney Island USA, the organization behind the Mermaid Parade, the Sideshow, and other throwback events.

For the uninitiated, Coney Island's best-known spots are just steps from the end of the D, F, N, and Q lines. Walking out of the station, you're immediately hit with the smell of salt air, the sight of Nathan's Famous in front of you, and the Wonder Wheel to your left.

to Coney Island-Stillwell Av

① *My Coney Island Baby.* Multifaceted artist Robert Wilson's mural, located in the Stillwell Avenue subway station, renders neighborhood icons—a kid on a carousel, a topping-laden hot-dog—in colorful glass bricks.

② **Nathan's Famous.** No visit is complete without a stop at this beachside staple. During the annual July 4th Hot Dog Eating Contest, competitors scarf down dozens of dogs in 10 minutes. (The current record: 69 franks.)

③ **Riegelmann Boardwalk.** This 2.7-mile-long boardwalk is jammed with people visiting its food stands, comfort stations, and various tchotchke shops.

④ **Coney Island Cyclone.** After eight decades, this coaster is still a beloved brain-rattler. Despite its ups and downs—we're not just talking about its 85-foot drop—the coaster remains one of Coney's most iconic attractions.

⑤ **The Coney Island Mermaid Parade.** Every June, this parade welcomes folks in nautical garb (think mermaids, crabs, and sailors) to the Boardwalk, and local luminaries are crowned King Neptune and Queen Mermaid.

⑥ **Totonno's.** Sample true New York pizza at this shop, a pillar of the Neopolitan slice since 1924. Its coal-fired pies, topped with tangy tomato sauce and creamy mozzarella, are as close to pizza nirvana as you'll find.

⑦ **Sideshows by the Seashore and Coney Island Museum.** These institutions hark back to the area's vaudevillian past with sideshows (you'll see a human blockhead), historical gems, and love for Coney's oddball side.

⑧ **MCU Park.** Minor league baseball thrives at this stadium, home of the Brooklyn Cyclones. Catch a game nearly every night during the summer, and don't miss the dazzling fireworks displays after weekend games.

⑨ **Ruby's Bar.** One of the city's last remaining dives, Ruby's is also one of the oldest institutions on the boardwalk. The 80-year-old bar offers no-frills food (burgers, fried seafood), cold beers, and plenty of vintage charm.

D F
N Q

5
FACTS
OFF THE

1. The Stillwell Avenue station is one of the transit system's greenest, with 2,730 solar panels forming a canopy over the tracks.

2. Don't let the name fool you: Coney Island is actually a peninsula, although it *was* once an island full of rabbits.

3. The 1979 cult classic *The Warriors* was filmed along Stillwell Avenue and the Boardwalk.

4. Every January 1, the Coney Island Polar Bear Club jumps into the frigid Atlantic to raise money for charity.

5. You won't find a Coney Island-style hot dog here; they originated in Michigan, not NYC.

ALONG THE WAY

●————————————●
W 8 St-NY Aquarium (F-Q)   86 St (N)

D **F**
N **Q**

The New York Aquarium. The stop is named for this aquatic attraction, located right across the street.

L&B Spumoni Gardens. Come for the delicious square slices, stay for the rich, namesake Italian ice cream.

THE **NEW YORK AQUARIUM**
FOUNDED IN 1896,
IS PART OF THE WILDLIFE
CONSERVATION SOCIETY, AN ORGANIZATION
ACTIVELY INVOLVED IN THE PROTECTION
OF CORAL REEFS FOR OUR AND FUTURE GENERATIONS.

1920
THE WONDER WHEEL,
A 150 FOOT TALL FERRIS WHEEL
OPENS AT CONEY ISLAND.

● Ocean Pkwy (Q)   ● Neptune Av (F)   ● Bay 50 St (D)

The Ocean Parkway Bike Path. Created in 1894, this was the first bike lane to open in the United States.

Looking Up. Artist Michael Krondl created this stained-glass piece as an impressionistic ode to the borough.

Calvert Vaux Park. This small green space faces Gravesend Bay, and is a prime spot to see ospreys.

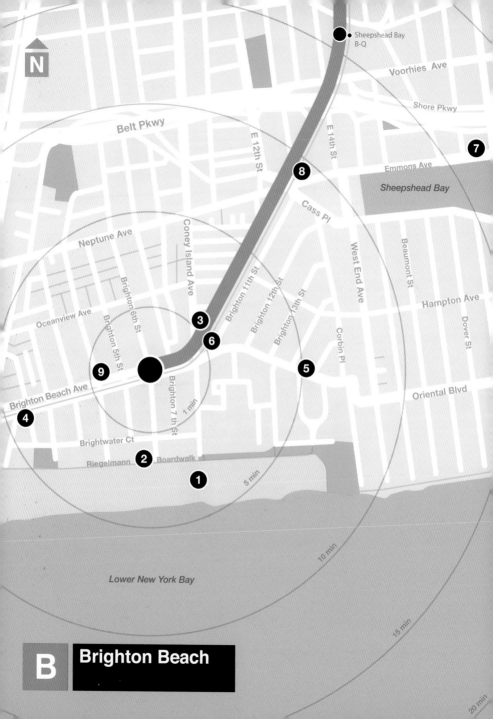

N

Sheepshead Bay
B-Q

Voorhies Ave

Shore Pkwy

Belt Pkwy

7

E 12th St

E 14th St

Emmons Ave

8

Sheepshead Bay

Cass Pl

West End Ave

Beaumont St

Neptune Ave

Coney Island Ave

Brighton 11th St

Brighton 12th St

Brighton 13th St

Hampton Ave

Oceanview Ave

Brighton 6th St

Brighton 5th St

3

6

Corbin Pl

Dover St

9

5

Brighton Beach Ave

Brighton 7 th St

1 min

Oriental Blvd

4

Brightwater Ct

2 Boardwalk

Riegelmann

1

5 min

Lower New York Bay

10 min

15 min

20 min

B **Brighton Beach**

to Brighton Beach

A trip to the end of the B line in Brighton Beach can be an utterly transportive experience—and not just because the eponymous subway stop is right by the Atlantic. Brighton is best known to New Yorkers as "Little Odessa," or the city's most vibrant Russian-speaking community, with immigrants from the Ukraine, Uzbekistan, and Russia itself all making their homes in the neighborhood.

Much like neighboring Coney Island, Brighton Beach was once a resort— even its name, after the seaside community in England, is meant to evoke the feeling of a retreat. Entrepreneur William Engeman built the first hotels and baths in the late 19th century, and soon, more businessmen followed suit. By the early 20th century, the neighborhood had numerous inns, waterfront attractions, and even several theaters, all of which led to a booming tourism industry.

The neighborhood's transformation into Little Odessa began in the mid-20th century, when Jewish immigrants from Europe first arrived in Brooklyn. Later, as immigration laws relaxed, more Russian-speaking people arrived in Brighton Beach, first in the '70s and again in the '90s. (Why Brighton in the first place? Allegedly, because of its similarity to the Black Sea.)

In recent years, another wave of immigrants—this time from Central Asian countries, like Uzbekistan and Kazakhstan—has made its way to Brighton Beach, bringing new cultural traditions and flavors to this unique microcosm of New York. Head to the end of the B to see for yourself.

to Brighton Beach

1 **Brighton Beach.** Less crowded than Coney Island, but not as exclusive as Manhattan Beach, the small strip of sand that makes up Brighton Beach is an ideal summertime destination.

2 **Tatiana Restaurant and Grill.** The food is almost beside the point at this Russian restaurant; on weekend evenings, a glitzy spectacle—there's fire, acrobatics, and dancing—takes over the space.

3 **Cafe Glechik.** The Ukrainian owners of this restaurant have imported the flavors of Odessa with dishes like *vareniki* (meat or potato-filled dumplings), hot or cold borscht, and chicken Kiev.

4 **Saint-Petersburg Global Trade House.** The Brighton Beach flagship of this mini-chain sells just about everything: Russian-language books, music and magazines, and decorative items (porcelain, Faberge-style eggs).

5 **Kashkar Cafe.** Named for a city on China's western edge, this restaurant is one of the few in NYC serving traditional Uyghur dishes, including kebabs, thick *lagman* (a type of noodle), and *dapanji,* a stewed chicken dish.

6 **Brighton Bazaar.** You'll find all manner of prepared foods at this Russian market, including potato pancakes, rye bread, Eastern European candies, and pickled *everything* (from vegetables to tongue to watermelon).

7 **Masal Cafe.** Try the traditional Turkish breakfast here, which comes with a boiled egg, various cheeses (including *labneh* and *kashkaval*), olives, and salami. Don't forget to have a cup of sweet Turkish coffee or tea.

8 **1001 Nights.** You'll find a mish-mash of Middle Eastern dishes at this lushly appointed restaurant, serving shish kebabs, *shurpa* (an Uzbek lamb soup), fried *manty* (a type of Central Asian dumpling), and more.

9 **Elza Fancy Food.** Also known as Cafe At Your Mother-in-Law, this might be NYC's only Korean-Uzbek restaurant. Dishes from both cultures are well represented, including *yug-gyada* (Korean beef soup) and pumpkin *samsa,* an Uzbek pastry.

B

5
FACTS
OFF THE

B

1. Brighton figures heavily in pop culture, from Neil Simon's *Brighton Beach Memoirs* to canceled reality show *Russian Dolls*.

2. Brighton was once home to comic-book legend Jack Kirby, songwriter Neil Sedaka, and Barbra Streisand.

3. If you're visiting Brighton Beach on a Sunday, take the Q train: though this is the end of the B, it doesn't stop there on weekends.

4. Über-patriotic composer John Philip Sousa played with a band at the Brighton Beach Music Hall at the turn of the 20th century.

5. Inventor Eben Moody Boynton debuted a monorail-like train from Gravesend to Brighton in 1878 but it never got off the ground.

ALONG THE WAY

Sheepshead Bay ● ——————————— ● Kings Hwy

B

Randazzo's Clam Bar. This waterfront Italian restaurant is known for its seafood, like lobster in a spicy tomato sauce.

Wyckoff Bennett Homestead. You'll have to view this 18th-century historic home from the outside, since it's not a museum.

Newkirk Plaza   **Cortelyou Rd (Q)**   **Church Av**

Bahar Masala. Take your pick from traditional Afghan dishes (*pulaow,* kofta kebabs) or halal Chinese eats at this spot.

Sycamore Bar. This homey pub (which once hosted indie rock band The National) has a cozy backyard and flowers for sale.

Prospect Park Parade Grounds. The southernmost end of Prospect Park is home to 40 acres of ball fields, where Sandy Koufax once played.

N

Henry Hudson Bridge

10 min

Inwood Hill Park

Indian Rd

W 218th St

6

5 min

W 215th St

Seaman Ave

Park Terrace E

1

9

8

215

5

1 min

Broadway

Seaman Ave

Cooper St

Payson Ave

Staff St

Dyckman St

4

W 211th St

2

3

W 212th St

Isham St

Henry Hudson Pkwy

Riverside Dr

W 207th St

W 204th St

Vermilyea Ave

Sherman Ave

207 St
1

9th Ave

7

Margaret Corbin Dr

Ft Tryon Pl

Dyckman St
A

Thayer St

Academy St

Post Ave

University Heights Bridg

W 206th St

Broadway

Dongan Pl

Dyckman St

W 205th St

10th Ave

W 204th St

Ellwood St

Arden St

Sickles St

W 203rd St

W 202nd St

Dyckman St
1

A | **Inwood**
207 St

to Inwood-207 St

Although it's a part of Manhattan, a visit to Inwood almost feels like taking a trip outside of New York City, thanks to its distance from Midtown's towering skyscrapers, as well as its acres of uninhabited terrain.

It's one of the city's most primeval enclaves thanks to Inwood Hill Park, whose salt marshes and forest are among the oldest in the city. A Native American tribe known as the Lenape, which occupied caves that remain in the park, once inhabited the land. (Inwood is also where, allegedly, Peter Minuit purchased Manhattan from the Lenape in 1626.) Despite the rapid development of New York City, Inwood Hill Park remains much the same as it did centuries ago.

The surrounding neighborhood, of course, has changed. Residential developments were scarce until a subway station opened on Dyckman Street in 1906, but once Inwood was accessible, people came in droves. The neighborhood was an Irish enclave for much of the 20th century, and a thriving Domincan community now calls it home. Recently, an influx of younger residents has upped Inwood's trendiness factor, but it remains a relatively undiscovered gem among NYC neighborhoods.

Exiting the subway at 207th Street and Broadway puts you smack in the middle of Inwood's main thoroughfare, which acts as something of a dividing line. To the east, the neighborhood is more industrial, with the elevated 1 train and an MTA rail yard hugging the Harlem River waterfront. West of Broadway, you'll find some of the area's most noteworthy landmarks, including its famous park.

to Inwood-207 St

1 **Inwood Hill Park.** There's more to see at this 196-acre space—including hiking trails, ballfields, and acres of forest—than you can fit in one trip. Muscota Marsh, a new enclave, overlooks the Henry Hudson Bridge.

2 **Dyckman Farmhouse Museum.** Completed in 1784 by William Dyckman (whose family was among the city's first Dutch settlers), this small farmhouse is now a museum dedicated to the family and life in 18th-century New York.

3 **Piper's Kilt.** Inwood's Irish population may be smaller now, but you can still get a juicy burger and a well-pulled pint of Guinness at this 24-year-old restaurant. Don't miss its unlimited boozy brunches on the weekends.

4 **Inwood Local.** The selection of craft beers at this laid-back bar is carefully curated, with several local options, and unlike many spots in the area, the kitchen in open until 1:00 AM.

5 **La Marina.** It didn't take long for this waterfront hot spot to become a trendy destination; Jay-Z and Beyoncé were even spotted there after it opened. Menu items can be pricey, but the view of the Hudson is unparalleled.

6 **Indian Road Cafe.** This cafe also serves as a community hub. Locally-sourced goodies are on the menu during the day. At night, there are plenty of events to choose from: trivia, live music, and cabaret shows.

7 **Fort Tryon Park.** The views of the Palisades from this park are worth the trip alone, but Fort Tryon is also home to the Cloisters, a medieval-style castle featuring elements that were transported brick-by-brick from France.

8 **West 215th St Steps.** This landmark would give Rocky Balboa a run for his money: more than 100 steps climb a hill from Broadway to Park Terrace East. Renovations will soon bring the century-old stairs into the 21st century.

9 **Inwood Greenmarket.** This year-round greenmarket brings New York farmstands, bakers, and wineries to the entrance of Inwood Hill Park. It's the perfect pit-stop to gather picnic supplies before spending a day at the green space.

A

1. Inwood isn't Manhattan's northernmost neighborhood; Marble Hill, on the same land mass as the Bronx, is.

2. At 230 feet above sea level, Inwood Hill is the second-highest point in Manhattan.

3. An MTA Arts & Design piece at the 207th St station marks the northern tip of the A line.

4. Famous Inwood residents, past and present, include playwright Lin-Manuel Miranda and basketball star Kareem Abdul-Jabbar.

5. A remnant of the grand Seaman-Drake Estate stands behind a Broadway auto-body shop.

ALONG THE WAY

● Dyckman St

● 190 St

Kenny Bakery. Try the cheap, strong cafe con leche at this spot, a neighborhood institution for more than 20 years.

190 St Subway. This station opened high atop a hill in 1932, and remains one of the deepest in the city.

181 St   **175 St**   **125 St**

181 Cabrini. Stop by this low-key Washington Heights bar for small plates or a glass of wine after a day of exploring.

Jeffrey's Hook Lighthouse. Also known as the Little Red Lighthouse, this landmark is the subject of a popular kids book.

Dinosaur Bar-B-Que. Fill up on mouth-watering barbecue specialties (brisket, ribs) and stick-to-your-ribs Southern sides.

N

Fort Washington
Park

J Hood
Wright Park

Hudson
River

Highbridge Park

Harlem
River

Fort Washington Ave
Haven Ave
Broadway
Wadsworth Ave
Audubon Ave
Amsterdam Ave
Harlem River Dr
Henry Hudson Pkwy
Edgecombe Ave
Jumel Pl
Amsterdam Ave
Major Deegan Expy
Harlem River Dr

181 St
1

175 St
A

W 176th St
W 175th St
W 174th St
W-172nd St
W 170th St
W 168th St
168 St
1
W 165th St
W 163rd St
W 161st St
W 160th St
W 159th St
157 St
1
168 St-
Amsterdam Av
C

① ⑧ ③ ⑥ ① ⑦ ⑨ ② ⑤ ④

1 min
5 min
10 min
15 min

C **168 St**

to 168 St

The end of the C doesn't quite feel like the end of anything; the 168 St stop is right in the middle of Washington Heights, and the stop itself is just another point on the A line up to Inwood. But exit at this station and you'll find one of Manhattan's most vibrant neighborhoods, with enough history and culture to fill an afternoon (or more).

The neighborhood takes its name from Fort Washington, in turn named for—of course—George Washington, whose Continental Army built the base during the Revolutionary War. (It would fall to the British during the Battle of Fort Washington in 1776.) Later, the land's Hudson River vistas would make it attractive to well-heeled New Yorkers. One of the biggest landmarks off the 168 St stop, the High Bridge, is more than 200 years old and was built as a conduit for the Old Croton Aqueduct.

Although Washington Heights developed in the early 20th century, things took a downturn in the '80s and '90s thanks, in part, to the crack epidemic that spread throughout New York City around that time. Crime rates soared, along with drug use; it would be more than a decade before the neighborhood began to bounce back. And bounce back it has: these days, Washington Heights is routinely namechecked as one of the city's safest neighborhoods.

There are many facets to the area: it's the city's biggest enclave for immigrants from the Dominican Republic, while vestiges of its heavily Irish and Greek past—not to mention its historical roots—remain.

to 168 St

1 **Coogan's.** This spot is more than just a bar; Coogan's is a local institution. It's frequented by politicians and celebrities, as well as Washington Heights residents and workers from nearby New York-Presbyterian hospital.

2 **Word Up Community Bookshop.** The word "community" in the name is intentional: In addition to selling used books, this tiny store hosts readings, film screenings, and other neighborhood-focused events.

3 **United Palace Theatre.** Originally opened in 1930 as a vaudeville house, this remains one of the city's most beautiful theaters, with opulent design touches. It now hosts live music, film screenings, and church services.

4 **Morris-Jumel Mansion.** During the Revolutionary War, George Washington used this house as his headquarters, and later, socialite Eliza Jumel lived there with her onetime husband Aaron Burr.

5 **Sylvan Terrace.** If you're visiting Morris-Jumel, detour along this tiny street, paved with Belgian blocks and lined with 19th-century clapboard homes. It was once used as a filming location for *Boardwalk Empire*.

6 **Highbridge Park.** A 116-foot-high crossing travels through this park, connecting the Bronx and Upper Manhattan. Another landmark, the Highbridge Water Tower, once provided water as part of the Old Croton Aqueduct Trail.

7 **Carrot Top Pastries.** True to its name, the specialty at this Washington Heights mainstay is the moist, dense carrot cake (made with real carrots), baked on-site every day and slathered in a cream cheese frosting.

8 **Malecon.** Though you'll find plenty of delicious Dominican specialties here (such as *quipes* and *sancocho*), the thing to order is the rotisserie chicken, which is roasted in the window and served with an addictive lime sauce.

9 **Malcolm X and Dr. Betty Shabazz Center**. The former site of the Audubon Ballroom, where the civil-rights leader was assassinated in 1965, this educational center now hosts talks, performances, and film screenings.

C

5 FACTS OFF THE C

1. American soldiers captured at the Battle of Fort Washington almost certainly ended up on the prison ships in New York Harbor.

2. Lin-Manuel Miranda's award-winning musical *In the Heights* is based on his experiences as a Washington Heights resident.

3. An ambitious plan to renovate the High Bridge will turn the crossing into a pedestrian pathway.

4. The 168th Street station complex was added to the National Register of Historic Places in 2005.

5. Although Audubon Avenue begins at 165th Street, John James Audubon's grand estate actually lies 10 blocks further south.

ALONG THE WAY

◯ 155 St   ◯ 145 St

Parlor Jazz at Marjorie Eliot's. For more than 20 years, Marjorie Eliot has hosted jazz musicians in her apartment, located in a historic building.

Jackie Robinson Park. Named for the groundbreaking baseball player, this park fittingly has a bust of Robinson at its entrance.

125 St

116 St

Cathedral Pkwy

Apollo Theatre. Harlem's most legendary venue has hosted the likes of James Brown, Michael Jackson, and Aretha Franklin, among many others.

Minton's. A former supper club that hosted jazz greats (Charlie Parker, Billie Holiday), the revived Minton's has live music most nights a week.

Cathedral Church of Saint John the Divine. This historic chapel offers weekly tours, including one that visits the roof.

N

Trinity
Cemetery

W 153rd St

Broadway

W 151st St

155 St
C

155 St
D

W 155th St

Riverside Dr

5

7

W 149th St

8

St Nicholas Ave

Edgecombe Ave

W 152nd St

Macombs Pl

Harlem River Dr

145 St
1

W 147th St

Amsterdam Ave

Convent Ave

St Nicholas Pl

9

Bradhurst Ave

W 150th St

W 145th St

W 148th St

1 min

3

W 143rd St

Hamilton Terrace

Frederick Douglass Blvd

Hamilton Pl

6

W 144th St

4

2

5 min

W 141st St

145 St
3

Amsterdam Ave

The City College
of New York

St Nicholas Terrace

Edgecombe Ave

Adam Clayton Powell Jr Blvd

W 135th St

1

135 St
B-C

10 min

W 138th St

5th Ave

W 135th St

W 139th St

W 137th St

B 3 Harlem-148 St
145 St

15 min

135 St
2-3

to 145 St / to Harlem-148 St

One of Harlem's toniest areas can be found near these two stops. The historic neighborhood of Hamilton Heights—named for the neighborhood's most famous resident, Alexander Hamilton—is situated at its southern end, while Sugar Hill, memorialized by the hip-hop group The Sugarhill Gang, is to the north of the 145 St subway stop.

Despite Alexander Hamilton's lengthy history in New York City, the house that bears his name was only his home for two years: He started construction on it in 1800, moved there in 1802, and was then killed in a duel with Aaron Burr in 1804. But the house, called the Grange, remained, and informed much of the character of the surrounding neighborhood—the pretty, block-long street across the way is even named Hamilton Terrace.

Sugar Hill, meanwhile, allegedly got its name because residents referred to living there as "the sweet life." It came into its own in the early 20th century, when wealthy African Americans moved into the beautiful homes lining streets like Convent Avenue and St. Nicholas Place. The neighborhood attracted plenty of notable names, including Thurgood Marshall, Langston Hughes, and Zora Neale Hurston; one building on Edgecombe Avenue alone was home to Duke Ellington, Lena Horne, and Count Basie.

Although the neighborhood has changed—there are more students these days, from Columbia University and otherwise—much of its historic charm remains. Exit at either of these stations and wander around, and you're mere blocks away from some of the prettiest real estate in all of Manhattan.

to 145 St / to Harlem-148 St

1 **St. Nicholas Park**. This 23-acre park is situated on a steep ridge, with City College perched at its summit. It's full of Manhattan schist, a type of bedrock, as well as migratory Monarch butterflies during mating season.

2 **Hamilton Grange National Memorial.** Alexander Hamilton lived in this stately home for two years. It stood near 143rd Street, then on Convent Avenue, before being placed in St. Nicholas Park in 2008.

3 ***The Royal Tenenbaums* House.** Though it's located on Archer Avenue in Wes Anderson's 2001 film, the home of the eccentric Tenenbaum family was this red-brick house on the corner of Convent Avenue and 144th Street.

4 **St. Luke's Episcopal Church**. This house of worship, with its grand Romanesque architecture, opened in the 1890s. A statue of Alexander Hamilton sits in its yard—fitting, since the church faces the Grange.

5 **Harlem Public.** This cozy hangout keeps things local, with NYC beers on tap, and décor touches—including pews from Mt. Moriah Church on 127th Street—that recall the area. The menu offers upscale pub grub.

6 **The Grange Bar & Eatery.** Opened by a husband-wife team who live in the neighborhood, the Grange—named for the Hamilton's home—serves farm-to-table fare, craft beer, and cocktails made with fresh juices.

7 **Maggie's Community Garden.** A verdant oasis amid West Harlem's hustle (it's situated just off of Broadway), this lovely community garden is named for Maggie Burnett, who has tended to the space for decades.

8 **Dance Theatre of Harlem.** Although the company here often performs at theaters in Manhattan, its Harlem headquarters hosts workshops, open performances, and classes for kids.

9 **Charles's Country Pan-Fried Chicken.** For more than 20 years, Charles Gabriel has been churning out succulent pan-fried chicken—made in a huge cast-iron pan, using his mother's recipe—to celebs and Harlem residents alike.

5 FACTS OFF THE B 3

1. City College was the first school that opened as part of the City University of New York system, in 1847.
2. The Grange sits across from Hamilton Terrace, a closed-off, one-block street named—yes, again—for Alexander Hamilton.
3. St. Nicholas Park and Avenue were named for St. Nicholas, dubbed the city's patron saint by New Yorker John Pintard.
4. Alexander Hamilton isn't the area's only famous name: Norman Rockwell and George Gershwin both lived in Hamilton Heights.
5. Convent Avenue is a beautiful old street—and it's exclusively residential, lacking any businesses whatsoever.

City College of New York.
Shepard Hall, one of the college's original buildings, is a landmark designed by George B. Post.

Levain Bakery. You can't go wrong with any of the baked goods here, but the chocolate chip cookies are rightly famous.

Cathedral Pkwy-110 St (B)   86 St (B)   81 St (B)

Central Park. The park's northernmost entrance is near the North Woods, the Lasker Rink, and more.

Prohibition. Bands perform nightly at this local hangout, serving punny cocktails ("Cool Hand Cuke") and pub grub.

American Museum of Natural History. This museum is famed for its planetarium, dinosaur fossils, and big blue whale.

to Times Sq-42 St

When most outsiders think of New York City, there's a good chance that Times Square is the first thing that comes to mind: the bright lights, the throngs of people, the neon marquees. But for locals, the relationship is more fraught; while plenty of New Yorkers pass through every day on their way to work or to the theater, many view it as an area to be avoided at all costs.

As long as it's been a neighborhood, Times Square has been given to extremes. High culture and low culture have always coexisted, with *The New York Times* headquarters and the opulent Astor Hotel located mere blocks from vaudeville theaters and brothels. Times Square became notorious in the later 20th century as a dangerous neighborhood, rampant with crime and seedy institutions; now, decades later, it's a glitzy, over-the-top tourist attraction. Like we said, extremes.

But there's no denying how significant a role it's played in shaping New York City's culture. Broadway theaters have thrived since the early 20th century, bringing thousands of visitors and aspiring actors to the city. The Brill Building, located at Broadway and 49th Street, was the nerve center of popular music in the mid-century, with songwriters like Carole King, Neil Diamond, and Jerry Leiber and Mike Stoller churning out hits there. And media outlets like MTV, *Good Morning America,* and Reuters have set up shop there, too.

Love it or loathe it, Times Square is a place that's worth a visit—and especially one that doesn't involve the Naked Cowboy. Even the most densely-packed parts of the neighborhood, like the area around the TKTS booth, have their charms. And if you venture off of Broadway, you'll find even more to love.

to Times Sq-42 St

① Father Duffy Square. Theater-lovers queue for cheap Broadway tickets at the red TKTS stairs at this plaza's center. A statue of Father Francis Patrick Duffy, a priest who tended to Broadway's elite, stands in front of the steps.

② Bryant Park. Once a potter's field, this park is now one of the city's prettiest green spaces, with a carousel, bocce court, and an expansive lawn. In the winter, a holiday market and ice-skating rink take over.

③ Kinokuniya Bookstore. Books, stationery, and Japanese tchotchkes (including tea accessories and toys) fill this multi-level space. On the second floor, you'll find a cafe selling Japanese sweets, teas, and lunch options.

④ Beer Authority. This tri-level pub has roughly 90 beers on tap, with selections to please both beer rubes and snobs. Skip the Bud and go for pours from Stone, Founders, and other craft purveyors.

⑤ Birdland. Named for iconic saxophonist Charlie Parker, this legendary jazz club still attracts the genre's heaviest hitters. Stop by on Sunday nights for regular sets from Arturo O'Farrill & The Afro-Latin Jazz Orchestra.

⑥ Playwrights Horizons. This esteemed theater has premiered work by Wendy Wasserstein, Stephen Sondheim (including *Assassins*), and Christopher Durang; you never know when a show here will be the next Broadway sensation.

⑦ The Town Hall. This McKim, Mead & White-designed theater also has a history as a political meeting place. Now, it hosts talks, live music, and other performances; come for a concert to experience its excellent acoustics.

⑧ One Times Square. Built a century ago as the headquarters of *The New York Times* (which stayed in the building for only a decade), this structure is now most famous as the location of the annual New Year's Eve ball drop.

⑨ Broadway theaters. Jukebox musicals and thought-provoking plays share space at the 40 designated Broadway theaters in operation. Ticket prices may be high, but the experience of seeing a show is unforgettable.

S 7

1. As of 2013, the Times Square subway stop was the busiest in the system, with an annual ridership of more than 63,000,000.

2. Several different subway lines pass through Times Square, but the 7 platform is the deepest one within the station.

3. The first New Year's Eve ball drop ball was a 700-pound heavyweight made of wood and iron.

4. The Times Square stop has the most MTA Arts & Design pieces with five installations, including a colorful Roy Lichtenstein mural.

5. The Lyceum Theatre on 45th Street claims to be Broadway's oldest theater, having hosted shows continuously since 1903.

ALONG THE WAY

Fifth Av (S-7)   Vernon Blvd-Jackson Av (7)

New York Public Library. Two stone lions, named Patience and Fortitude, stand guard at the entrance to this Beaux Arts building on Fifth Avenue.

Alewife NYC. Craft-beer fans will have plenty to choose from at this pub, which offers dozens of global brews.

Queensboro Plaza (7)   **46 St-Bliss St (7)**   **69 St (7)**

Silvercup Studios. Many series that film in NYC, including *30 Rock* and *Orange is the New Black*, have set up shop here.

"Welcome to Sunnyside" sign. The 30-year-old Art Deco sign is an iconic entry point to this diverse neighborhood.

Sripraphai Thai. Often namechecked as one of the city's best Thai restaurants, this Woodside spot offers regional specialties.

N

47-50 Sts
Rockefeller Ctr
B-D-F-M

W 48th St

E 50th St

6th Ave

W 44th St

5th Ave

Madison Ave

Park Ave

W 43rd St

42 St-Bryant Pk
B-D-F-M

Bryant Park

5 Av
7

2

1

E 44th St

8

6

7

42nd St

E 43rd St

9

W 38th St

E 40th St

Grand Central-
42 St
4-5-6
1 min

Grand Central-
42 St
7

E 39th St

W 36th St

E 37th St

5

E 35th St

4

3

Park Avenue

5 min

Lexington Ave

3rd Ave

E 40th St

5th Ave

Madison Ave

E 35th St

E 36th St

E 38th St

2nd Ave

10 min

S **Grand Central**
42 St

to Grand Central-42 St

No discussion of New York City's biggest landmarks is complete without mentioning Grand Central Terminal. The Beaux Arts structure was a sensation when it opened in 1913, and has remained one of the city's most visited buildings—and that's not just because this subway stop, where the 42nd Street Shuttle ends, is the second most popular in the subway system.

Before the current building was erected, a train depot opened in 1871 on the same site. Demand quickly outpaced space, and the station was so reviled that *The New York Times* referred to it as "a cruel disgrace." A number of factors—including a fatal crash in the Park Avenue tunnel in 1902—led to the terminal's reconstruction, with the beautiful structure used today opening nearly a decade later.

Grand Central's reopening was a boon for Midtown, bringing more commuters, businesses, and day-trippers to the area—it even led to the construction of landmarks like the nearby Chrysler and Helmsley Buildings. The station itself quickly became a destination in its own right, with tourists clamoring to see the main concourse's sky-high ceiling, or the gorgeous Guastavino tiled arches that can be found throughout.

Now, Grand Central is one of the busiest train stations in the country (along with Penn Station across town), but its grandeur hasn't changed over the years. (The same can't be said for Penn Station.) You could spend a day inside the terminal alone, but be sure to venture outside to see what else Midtown has to offer.

to Grand Central-42 St

① Grand Central Terminal. Few experiences compare to that of standing in the main lobby of this station and gazing up at its constellation-covered ceiling. Be careful at midday, when commuters pack the space.

② New York Transit Museum Annex. Like its Brooklyn counterpart, this rail-focused museum is located in a train depot (on the main level of Grand Central Terminal). Its most popular exhibit is the annual Holiday Train Show.

③ The Morgan Library & Museum. Once the home of legendary financier J.P. Morgan, the complex also includes a library designed by McKim, Mead & White, and an entrance by Renzo Piano that was added in 2006.

④ The Ginger Man. On weeknights, be prepared to face happy-hour crowds at this bar; the 200-plus beer options make it worth it. Try the Ginger Man Ale, created by Captain Lawrence Brewing Company for the bar.

⑤ Art on Park Avenue. Each year, the nonprofit Fund for Park Avenue places sculptures in the median strip along Park Avenue. Artists like Tom Otterness and Robert Indiana have shown work there, and it's free to see.

⑥ Grand Central Oyster Bar. Open for more than a century, this subterranean seafood restaurant is an excellent spot to grab a martini, a plate of raw bivalves, and the delectable oyster pan roast.

⑦ Grand Central Market. New York institutions like Zabar's, Murray's Cheese, and Li-Lac Chocolates all pack into this space, one of the best spots to grab a snack before catching your train.

⑧ The Campbell Apartment. Hidden in a corner of the station, this lounge, once the office of a '20s magnate, serves period-appropriate cocktails. The Prohibition Punch combines rum, fresh juices, and champagne.

⑨ Chrysler Building. This iconic 1,046-foot-tall building, completed in 1930, was NYC's tallest until the Empire State Building opened. Its Art Deco design and ornamentation make it perhaps the most beautiful building in New York.

5
FACTS
OFF THE

S

1. A hidden track—no. 61—was used by President Franklin Roosevelt to travel between Grand Central and the Waldorf Astoria Hotel.

2. At the "whispering gallery" on the lower level, couples can stand on either side and hear each other's soft whispers.

3. A hidden underground bunker called M42 contains a power grid for the entire station.

4. The star mural on the terminal's ceiling was painted backwards—possibly on purpose, according to the Vanderbilts.

5. When Grand Central opened in 1913, 150,000 people visited the station; now more than 700,000 commuters pass through daily.

Bookmarks Lounge. Situated atop the Library Hotel, this literary-themed bar offers drinks named for Ernest Hemingway and Jackie Collins.

The Algonquin Hotel. Have a drink at this storied writer's hangout—there is, of course, a cocktail named for Dorothy Parker.

LAMBS ROOM →

LANGTRY ROOM →

BULL MOOSE ROOM →

N ROOM →

5 Av   5 Av   5 Av

Keens Steakhouse. Notable names like Babe Ruth visited this classic chophouse, which is largely unchanged from its 1885 origins.

The Roosevelt Hotel. Named for President Theodore Roosevelt, this 1920s hotel has since been featured on the television series *Mad Men*.

Kati Roll Company. The handheld kati rolls served here come with flavorful fillings, like chicken tikka or spicy potato.

N

W 23rd St

23 St
C-E

W 20th St

W 21st St

W 18th St

W 22nd St

23 St
1

11th Ave

9th Ave

W 16th St

W 19th St

8th Ave

7th Ave

W 15th St

2

14 St
A-C-E

18 St
1

1

Gansevoort St

W 13th St

W 16th St

3

W 17th St

Horatio St

Greenwich Ave

W 15th St

14 St
1-2-3

14 St
F-M

1 min

Jane St

8

4

Hudson
River

7

W 12th St

W 13th St

Bethune St

Bank St

Waverly Pl

W 11th St

6 Av
L

5 min

5

Perry St

Hudson St

Charles St

W 12th St

10 min

6

W 10th St

West St

W 10th St

W 8th St

5th Ave

9

Christopher St-
Sheridan Sq
1

Christopher St

15 min

W 4 St-Wash Sq
A-B-C-D-F-M

Barrow St

Washington
Square Park

L 8 Av

Carmine St

to 8 Av

Situated at the crossroads of the West Village, the Meatpacking District, and Chelsea, this station lets passengers out into a wholly changed neighborhood. Thanks to the development of luxury hotels, trendy restaurants, and, more recently, the High Line, what was once an industrial center has turned into one of New York's swankest areas.

It wasn't always like this. The West Village, to the south, was long a bohemian enclave; it was also the home of Jane Jacobs, the great defender of diverse neighborhoods. Recently, luxury chains and wealthier residents have moved in, meaning some of that diverse character has been lost. Similarly, the once-industrial Chelsea, which became a haven for artists and a thriving LGBT community, is becoming ritzier.

The change was even more drastic in the Meatpacking District, to the west. Slaughterhouses once dominated the area (hence the name), with the elevated railway along Tenth Avenue used to transport cattle. Now, that railway is the High Line, which opened in 2009 and has transformed the surrounding area. Even before then, an influx of trendy clubs and hotels (such as the Hotel Gansevoort) had created a hub for nightlife. But thanks to the High Line's popularity, more change (in the form of luxury buildings and high-end shops and restaurants) is coming.

Despite all this, there's plenty to champion in the area; the High Line is, to be fair, one of the city's great urban innovations. The charming streets, beautiful architecture, and even some of that bohemian feel that has attracted visitors to the area for decades remains; you just have to know where to look.

to 8 Av

1 **The High Line.** This park has become one of NYC's most popular green spaces. Built on a former elevated railway, it features art projects, well-manicured flora, and restaurants—try Terroir, a wine bar with small plates.

2 **Chelsea Market.** Once a Nabisco factory, this bazaar is full of excellent places to eat and shop. Grab a latte at Ninth Street Espresso, biscuits at Amy's Bread, or tacos (try the marinated pork) at Los Tacos No. 1.

3 **Rubin Museum of Art.** Himalayan art is the focus at this small museum, which showcases artifacts from Tibet, Nepal, and other far-flung countries. Public programs include mind-bending lectures and a weekly happy hour.

4 **NYC Pride.** Every summer, the West Village becomes the epicenter of New York's LGBT pride festivities, including rallies, celebratory parties, dances, and more. The Pride March also ends in the neighborhood.

5 **The Meatball Shop.** This minichain specializes in—you guessed it—meatballs, serving varieties like classic beef or spicy pork with your choice of sauce. Don't miss the huge, house-made ice cream sandwiches.

6 **Three Lives & Company.** This cozy bookstore first opened in 1968, and has thrived in the years since thanks to its friendly, knowledgeable staff. Let them guide you through sections devoted to poetry, fiction, and more.

7 **Abingdon Square Park.** One of the West Village's prettiest parks, this triangular space is bordered by trees, and has a statue dedicated to New Yorkers who fought during World War I at its center.

8 **Corner Bistro.** Little has changed at this tavern since it opened half a century ago, including the burger, which still comes with American cheese and bacon. Wash it down with a mug of McSorley's Ale.

9 **Hudson River Park.** This waterfront park stretches along Manhattan's west side, with some of its nicest amenities—including Pier 51's play area, and the lawn at 14th Street park—in the area. The protected bike path is one of the city's best.

L

1. Artist Tom Otterness installed tiny bronze sculptures, including an alligator climbing out of a manhole, throughout the L station.

2. The West Village has long been used as a film and TV setting, including for *Sex and the City, Friends,* and *When Harry Met Sally.*

3. At 2.3 miles long, 14th Street is the longest crosstown street in Manhattan, connecting the Hudson and East Rivers.

4. The Westbeth Artists Community on Bethune Street was once a Bell Laboratories outpost where the transistor was invented.

5. The Commissioner's Plan of 1811 did not include the West Village—that's why its streets are so confusing.

ALONG THE WAY

6 Av

14 St-Union Sq

Murray's Bagels. Grab a classic NYC nosh—a hand-rolled bagel with lox and a schmear—at this small delicatessen.

The Strand Bookstore. Let yourself get lost amid 18 miles of books—new, used, and everything in between—at this iconic bookstore.

F BOOKS

AND

STORE

●
3 Av

●
1 Av

●
Bedford Av

Momofuku Milk Bar. Christina Tosi's desserts, including the salty-sweet-buttery Crack Pie, are the stars of this Momofuku offshoot.

Academy Records. This small shop specializes in vinyl records; set aside a few hours to dig through crates.

Vinnie's Pizzeria. Get a delicious plain slice; or better yet, order one of the specials, listed on a cartoon- and pun-filled whiteboard.

N

Canal St
4-6

Canal St
J-Z

Canal St
N-Q

White St

5 min

Worth St

Chambers St
1-2-3

Broadway

1 min

9

Bayard St

Mott St

Pell St

8

Worth St

6

Chambers St
A-C

7

Chambers St

2

City Hall
N-R

1

Park Pl
2-3

5

3

Chambers St
J-Z

4

Madison St

St James Pl

Fulton St

Spruce St

Ann St

Fulton St
A-C

Fulton St
J-Z

Fulton St
4-5

Fulton St
2-3

Brooklyn Bridge

Catherine Slip

John St

Pearl St

FDR Drive

East
River

6 **Brooklyn Bridge
City Hall**

to Brooklyn Bridge-City Hall

History is written throughout New York City's five boroughs, but for the past two centuries, New York's civic center has been located just off of this subway stop. The subway station may be named after City Hall, but the Tweed Courthouse and the Municipal Building, home to the Manhattan Borough President's and City Clerk's offices, are also nearby.

But this area is important for another reason: It's where the New York City subway system began in 1904, with the first nine-mile-long Interborough Rapid Transit line operating between City Hall and 145th Street. The old City Hall station was the first to open, and its design—with chandeliers, skylights, and tiled archways—was uncommonly refined, a style that hasn't been seen in a subway stop since.

Though this particular part of town is dense with history, its dining and nightlife options are less than robust. But head a few blocks north and cross Worth Street, and you'll find yourself on the outskirts of Chinatown, the best-known and oldest of the city's Chinese enclaves. The development of the Lower East Side has threatened to change the landscape of the neighborhood, but for now, many of its Chinese markets, restaurants, and businesses remain, and are worth a trip.

Armed with that knowledge, it's easy to plan an outing along the end of the 6. History buffs can stick with the area around City Hall, and gawk at the newly-married couples posing for photos outside of the Municipal Building. Farther north, you can explore one of the city's most densely populated and interesting neighborhoods.

to Brooklyn Bridge-City Hall

(1) New York City Hall. This majestic building opened in 1812, and remains the seat of New York City government. It's home to both the Mayor's Office and the City Council, and is surrounded by other municipal offices.

(2) City Hall Park. This space attracts municipal workers and other downtown denizens. A large fountain by architect Jacob Wrey Mould is one focal point, while public art projects and monuments are scattered throughout.

(3) Old City Hall stop. If you're on a downtown 6 train, don't get off at City Hall; instead, stay on as it moves to the uptown track to catch a glimpse of the old City Hall stop from 1904, renowned for its gorgeous architecture.

(4) Brooklyn Bridge. This East River crossing opened in 1883 and became an immediate sensation. The allure has yet to fade, with thousands walking its span (and posing under its Gothic arches) every day.

(5) Woolworth Building. Once the tallest skyscraper in New York City (until the Chrysler Building, anyway), Cass Gilbert's beauty is considered an architectural gem. See his ornate work for yourself on a public tour.

(6) African Burial Ground. This was a cemetery for free and enslaved Africans in the 17th and 18th centuries. The remains of more than 400 people were reinterred there in 2003, and it became a National Monument in 2006.

(7) Fountain Pen Hospital. This unique shop—devoted, as the name suggests, to selling and repairing fountain pens—has a faithful clientele. Stop by to check out the wares, including pens made from gold or diamond.

(8) Joe's Shanghai. This Chinatown restaurant is famous for its soup dumplings, a Shanghai delicacy. Choose either pork or crab; when your food arrives, bite a small hole to release the broth first, then dig in.

(9) Chinatown Ice Cream Factory. This ice cream shop has been serving inventive, Asian-inspired desserts for more than 30 years, with flavors like lychee, black sesame, and even durian (the pungent Southeast Asian fruit).

6

1. This isn't New York's original City Hall; that was located closer to South Street Seaport, in the heart of New Amsterdam.

2. John Roebling designed the Brooklyn Bridge, but his daughter-in-law, Emily, oversaw construction after his death in 1869.

3. After President Abraham Lincoln was killed, his body lay in state at City Hall on its journey from Washington, D.C. to Illinois.

4. Marc Gibian's MTA Arts & Design piece, *Cable Crossing* (in the City Hall stop) echoes the steel cables of the Brooklyn Bridge.

5. The unpopular statue *Civic Virtue,* with a man (virtue) stepping on two women (vice), was first installed in City Hall Park in 1922.

美國華人博物

ALONG THE WAY

Canal St   Spring St

6

Museum of Chinese in America. Maya Lin designed the building for this institution devoted to Chinese history.

Jack's Wife Freda. Mediterranean-inspired comfort food draws crowds to this small, homey restaurant.

Bleecker St   **Astor Pl**   **23 St**

Bowery Arts & Science. This organization runs the Bowery Poetry Club, one of the city's oldest alt-arts venues.

Joe's Pub. Part of the Public Theater complex, this venue hosts cabaret acts, live music, and other funky performances.

Eleven Madison Park. Dinner here is a splurge, but worth it: the local, seasonal tasting menu changes each night.

N

Franklin St
1

N Moore St

10 min

River Terrace

West St

Greenwich St

Worth St

5 min

Warren St

Chambers St
1-2-3

9

North End Ave

Murray St

4

6

Chambers St

Broadway

8

5

Vesey St

Chambers St
A-C

W Broadway

Barclay St

1 min

1

Park Pl
2-3

City Hall
R

North
Cove
Yacht
Harbor

7

West St

North
Pool

World Trade
Center

2

3

Fulton St

South End Ave

South
Pool

Cortlandt St
N-R

Dey St

Fulton St
A-C

Fulton St
J-Z

Ann St

Spruce

Cortlandt St

Liberty St

Thirty Pl

Fulton St
4-5

Fulton St
2-3

Maiden Ln

John St

E **World Trade Center**

to World Trade Center

When it comes to the area around the World Trade Center stop, its development can be split into "before" and "after," with 9/11 as the catastrophic dividing point. Although the neighborhood has rebounded—it's now among the most-visited parts of in the city—getting there wasn't easy.

Intended to boost the economic development of Lower Manhattan, the original World Trade Center campus, including the iconic Twin Towers, opened in the early 1970s. Around the same time, construction began on Battery Park City, a planned community that made the Hudson River waterfront into a real neighborhood. (It's built on land that was created, in part, by using debris from the World Trade Center site.) For decades, the area thrived as a commercial hub.

But after 9/11, the neighborhood was utterly transformed. In the aftermath of the tragedy, the city and state governments came together to rebuild. Organizations like the Lower Manhattan Development Corporation and the Downtown Alliance have worked to help revitalize the area, and the National September 11 Memorial Foundation (responsible for the memorial and museum) was created not long after the attacks. Slowly but surely, Lower Manhattan began to recover.

Now, more than a decade after 9/11, the neighborhood is once again transformed. The new World Trade Center campus is being rebuilt as an open, public plaza. There are more housing and retail options than ever before, and the population is higher than it was in 2000. At this point, it's fair to say that the area has bounced back.

to World Trade Center

1 **One World Trade Center.** The 1,776-foot-tall building is the anchor of the WTC campus and is among the tallest buildings in the world. A public observatory, located on the 100th floor, offers panoramic views of the city.

2 **National September 11 Memorial & Museum.** Built to commemorate the 9/11 attacks, this institution includes both a museum and the memorial plaza, with reflecting pools built in the footprint of the former Twin Towers.

3 **St. Paul's Chapel.** Part of Trinity Church, this chapel has lasted through several disasters, including the Great Fire of 1776 and 9/11 centuries later. Also a rich historical site, it's home to a pew that George Washington used.

4 **Francois Payard Bakery.** A more casual outpost of the titular chef's Upper East Side patisserie, this café serves not only Payard's famed pastries, but also panini, salads, and quiches.

5 **Shake Shack.** Danny Meyer's near-ubiquitous burger chain offers the same delicious burgers, hot dogs, and frozen custard as its other NYC outposts, along with location-specific touches, such as a Wall-nut Street concrete.

6 **The Mysterious Bookshop.** Originally opened in 1979, this indie bookseller is devoted to thrillers, crime stories, and whodunits. The shop also hosts book clubs focused on topics like hard-boiled thrillers or historical mysteries.

7 **Brookfield Place.** It's easy to stay entertained at this public space: There are more than a dozen restaurants (including an Umami Burger) and a robust cultural calendar filled with live music, art installations, and more.

8 **Irish Hunger Memorial.** This tribute to the Great Irish Famine is meant to evoke the Irish landscape, with native limestone and plants imported from the Emerald Isle, and pieces of an actual cottage from County Mayo.

9 **Nelson A. Rockefeller Park.** In warmer months, this space is filled with crowds picnicking, playing sports, or soaking up the sun. Part of Battery Park City, its Hudson River views make it a perennially popular spot.

E

1. The E stop will soon be part of the larger WTC transportation hub, which includes Santiago Calatrava's *Oculus* sculpture.

2. Until 1976, the E ran into Brooklyn, with service ending in the Rockaways; that service was later replaced by the C train.

3. Philippe Petit tightrope-walked between the Twin Towers in 1974, while base-jumpers leapt from 1WTC in 2013.

4. In 1978, Creative Time staged an installation called *Art On the Beach* on the landfill that later became Battery Park City.

5. Radio Row, a small business district along Cortlandt and Dey Streets, was razed to make room for the World Trade Center.

Nancy Whiskey Pub. This dive opens as early as 11AM some days, giving patrons more time to down cheap beers and play shuffleboard.

Dominique Ansel Bakery. French chef Ansel is known for creating the Cronut, but any of his confections are worth a try.

W 4 St-Wash Sq   23 St   34 St-Penn Station

Comedy Cellar. Famous comedians, including Dave Chappelle and Jerry Seinfeld, regularly grace this subterranean club's stage.

Doughnut Plant. Creative, delicious doughnuts (try the moist tres leches variety) are available all day at this bakery.

Tracks Raw Bar & Grill. A raw bar in Penn Station? Believe it: This pub, located near the LIRR, is beloved by commuters.

to Broad St

If you look at Lower Manhattan, the history of the city can be traced, in some ways, to different ends of subway lines. South Ferry, for example, is close to where New Amsterdam was founded, while the city's government is headquartered around the end of the 6 at Brooklyn Bridge-City Hall. As for Broad St, its location—right next to the New York Stock Exchange—puts it smack in the middle of where the city's financial history was written.

The beginnings of that moneyed era can be traced back to 1792, when "the Buttonwood Agreement" was signed on Wall Street. There, 24 stockbrokers agreed to trade only with each other, establishing the city's first New York Stock Exchange. In the years since then, more financial institutions— including the Bank of New York (founded, in part, by Alexander Hamilton) and the Federal Reserve Bank of New York—came to the area, leading to the neighborhood being called the Financial District.

But the area's history isn't limited to money: The site where George Washington was sworn in as president is now Federal Hall, a National Memorial that's catty-corner to the Stock Exchange; and landmarks like Bowling Green, Battery Park, and the World Trade Center aren't too far away. And there are, of course, links to New York's present, including museums that showcase the history of the area.

Like many of the ends of line in Lower Manhattan, Broad St is intimately connected to New York's past. And if you're interested in the rich capitalist history of the United States—and how it connects to New York City—then this subway stop is the best place to start.

to Broad St

1   **Federal Hall.** In 1789, George Washington was sworn in as president on this site. Though the building where he took the oath was torn down, the current structure remains a memorial to America's early history.

2   **New York Stock Exchange.** Members of the public can't actually see the NYSE trading floor, but that doesn't stop visitors from admiring the stately Neoclassical building, decorated with an American flag, from the outside.

3   **Museum of American Finance.** Not far from NYSE, this museum holds artifacts chronicling America's financial history. The building was the former headquarters of the Bank of New York.

4   **Trinity Church Wall Street.** After Alexander Hamilton was killed during a duel with Aaron Burr, he was buried in the cemetery next to Trinity Church. The 150-year-old church building is a landmark in its own right.

5   **Stone Street.** This quaint road (called Brewer Street in the 17th-century) was one of the city's first paved streets. Now, it's home to several pubs, including the Irish bar Ulysses, and craft-beer haven the Growler.

6   **Delmonico's.** This 178-year-old restaurant, the first fine-dining spot in America, was once namechecked by Edith Wharton and F. Scott Fitzgerald. Dishes created there include lobster Newburg and baked Alaska.

7   **77 Water St.** This is one of the area's oddest buildings: A small, old-timey candy shop operates out of its lobby, while a replica of a World War I fighter plane can be spotted on the roof. (The owners placed it there for kicks.)

8   **Bluestone Lane Coffee.** Hidden on a side street, this Australian coffee shop specializes in treats that are popular Down Under, including strong Flat Whites (espresso with steamed milk) and smashed avocado on toast.

9   **Museum of Jewish Heritage.** Exhibitions at this institution focus on modern Jewish history and the aftermath of the Holocaust. The outdoor installation *Garden of Stones,* by Andy Goldsworthy, is intended to be a living memorial.

J   Z

1. In 1653, Dutch colonists built a wall to protect New Amsterdam from the British; today, that location is Wall Street.

2. If you look at the façade of 23 Wall Street, you can still see marks from a bombing that happened in 1920 at Wall and Broad Streets.

3. A semi-secret underground passage connects Broad Street to the 2/3 and the 4/5 at Wall Street, as well as buildings.

4. There's a Manhattan oddity close to the subway: Marketfield Street, one of only a few remaining L-shaped alleyways in the borough.

5. Walk to Broadway to see the Canyon of Heroes, plaques embedded in the sidewalk marking various ticker-tape parades.

ALONG THE WAY

● Fulton St

● Canal St

Theater Alley. This historic block was once home to the Park Theatre, a wildly popular venue; now, it's simply a small cobblestone block.

Nom Wah Tea Parlor. Originally built in 1920, this dim sum spot was restored to its full vintage glory in 2010.

| Bowery | Essex St | Marcy Av |

Bowery Ballroom. One of the city's best venues for live music, this intimate club hosts both major acts and up-and-comers.

Tenement Museum. Through tours of re-created early-20th-century apartments, this museum offers a glimpse into the history of the Lower East Side.

Peter Luger Steak House. Sample classic dishes—creamed spinach, grilled thick-cut bacon, and, of course, steak—at this storied chophouse.

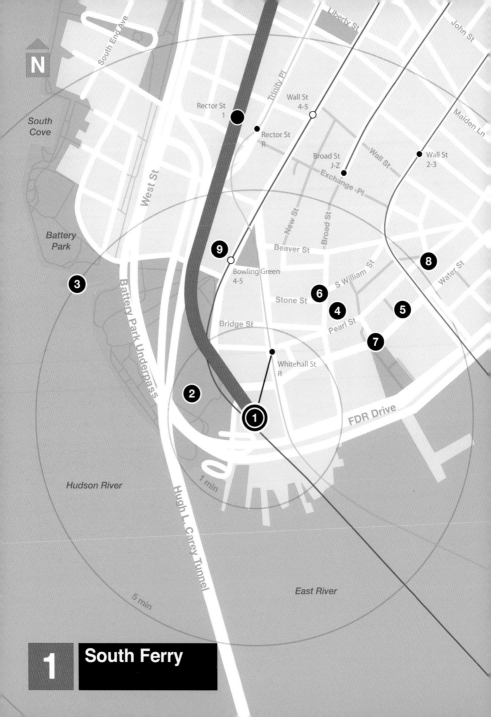

N

South Cove

Rector St
1

Rector St
R

Wall St
4-5

Broad St
J-Z

Exchange Pl

Wall St

Maiden Ln

Wall St
2-3

West St

Battery Park

New St

Broad St

Beaver St

Bowling Green
4-5

S William St

Stone St

Water St

Battery Park Underpass

Bridge St

Pearl St

Whitehall St
R

FDR Drive

Hudson River

Hugh L. Carey Tunnel

1 min

5 min

East River

1 **South Ferry**

to South Ferry

Positioned at Manhattan's southernmost tip, the South Ferry stop is on particularly fertile ground. When Dutch colonists founded New Amsterdam in the 17th century, the city was clustered around the waterfront, with Wall Street acting as its northern border. (When the MTA excavated what would become the new South Ferry station, they discovered thousands of artifacts, including pottery, shoes, and animal bones.)

As the city continued to grow and develop, South Ferry remained a vital commercial hub. In 1905, the city assumed operation of the Staten Island Ferry; a century later, a brand-new ferry terminal opened, with an airy lobby and—crucially—an easier connection to a new subway terminal, which by then was well underway.

When that stop opened in 2009, commuters rejoiced—finally, the old station, originally built in 1905, would be replaced. But that was short-lived: in 2012, Hurricane Sandy flooded the whole thing, ruining equipment, tunnels, and even escalators and paint jobs. Although the MTA plans to rebuild the station, it will be years before it's complete; as of 2013, the 1 train returned to the old stop.

Despite the setback, South Ferry is still a hugely popular stop, both with locals working downtown, and tourists seeking easy access to Lower Manhattan's tourist attractions (it's close to Bowling Green, Battery Park, and the Statue of Liberty ferries, to name a few). It's a perfect spot to start any exploration of old New York City.

to South Ferry

1 **Staten Island Ferry Whitehall Terminal.** Each year, more than 22 million travelers pass through this hub to ride the Staten Island Ferry, and for good reason: the ride is free and offers some of the best views of the city.

2 **Battery Park.** Like the song says, the Bronx is up and the Battery is down—way down, at the southern point of Manhattan. This park is home to monuments, museums, and art installations, and has gorgeous views to boot.

3 **Pier A Harbor House.** A 19th-century government building at the foot of Manhattan was recently converted into a gigantic rathskeller, serving beers and other spirits, bar snacks, oysters, and more gustatory delights.

4 **The Dead Rabbit.** This award-winning saloon—named for an infamous 19th-century Irish gang—looks to the past with its expansive cocktail menu, with drinks inspired by long-forgotten recipes.

5 **Elevated Acre.** True oases are hard to come by in Manhattan, but this small park—an acre of land perched above the East River—qualifies, offering a respite from the noise below. In the summer, catch movie screenings.

6 **Fraunces Tavern.** On the site of George Washington's final address to the Continental Army's officers, you'll find a Revolutionary War museum, fine-dining restaurant, and a whiskey bar.

7 **Vietnam Veterans Plaza.** Opened in 1985 and renovated following 9/11, this peaceful space honoring New Yorkers who fought in the Vietnam War features a reflecting fountain and a memorial with the names of the dead.

8 **Souvlaki GR.** Before this Greek eatery had a restaurant, there was its food truck, which can still be found regularly at Hanover and Water Streets. Try the addictive SGR pita, stuffed with grilled chicken, spicy feta, and fries.

9 **National Museum of the American Indian.** The former Alexander Hamilton U.S. Customs House is now home to this Smithsonian institution, which collects artwork, historical artifacts, and clothing from Native peoples in the Western Hemisphere.

1. The Staten Island Ferry wasn't always free; until 1997, a round-trip ride would cost you 50 cents.

2. The *Charging Bull* statue was first placed, without permission, near the Stock Exchange in 1989.

3. Passengers exiting the 1 at South Ferry must be in the first five cars of the train; the track is too short to allow more cars in.

4. The plaza outside of the ferry terminal is named for Peter Minuit, who allegedly purchased Manhattan from the Lenape in 1626.

5. *The Sphere,* a sculpture from the old World Trade Center that survived the collapse of the Twin Towers, is located in Battery Park.

ALONG THE WAY

Rector St   Franklin St

3LD Art & Technology Center.
Run by the 3-Legged Dog
Theater Group, this space
hosts innovative multimedia
performances.

Urban Archaeology. This shop's
owners scour historic sites for
its selection of restored and
salvaged antiques.

Canal St   **Houston St**   **Christopher St-Sheridan Sq**

Albert Capsouto Park. Named for a local activist, this peaceful space has a waterfall and plenty of seating.

Film Forum. New York's best movie theater is this three-screen gem that shows indie flicks and classic films.

Stonewall Inn. This cozy bar, a linchpin of the LGBT rights movement, is still going strong.

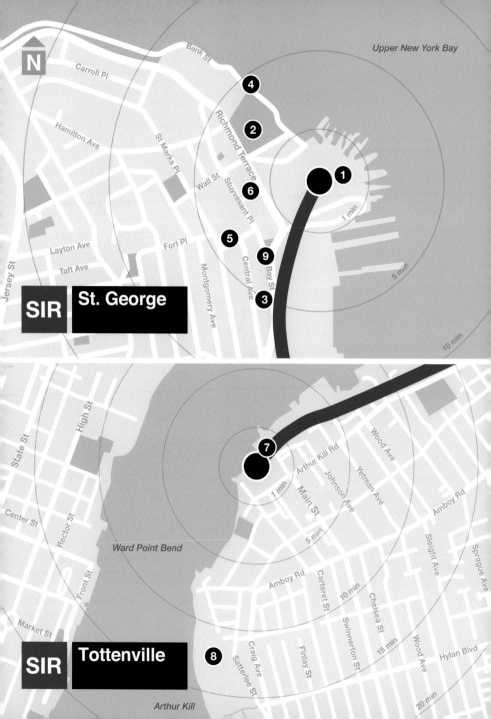

to St. George and Tottenville

Visitors to New York City won't casually find themselves on the Staten Island Railway. After all, it's entirely contained within Staten Island, with no connection to the other four boroughs aside from the Staten Island Ferry. You have to make an effort to get to the SIR—and it's worth the trip, especially if you've never visited Staten Island before.

The northern end of the SIR is the St. George stop, close to the Staten Island Ferry. This part of the island is also relatively packed with things to do: the Richmond County Bank Ballpark, home to the Staten Island Yankees, is a short walk from the ferry terminal, and the neighborhood of St. George is teeming with restaurants, bars, and cultural spots. (And soon, it'll be home to the New York Wheel, a gigantic observation wheel scheduled to open in 2017.)

If you take the 45-minute SIR ride to Tottenville, at the southern end of the island, you'll find an entirely different Staten Island. Tottenville is a largely residential neighborhood, with shops and restaurants clustered around a few main thoroughfares. The southernmost tip of the island is home to Conference Park, a peaceful green space overlooking Arthur Kill. The streets are lined with beautiful homes, some of which date back to the 19th century, and the small community is more like a suburb than a part of New York City.

The trip between the two stops is perhaps the most unusual in the subway system. The SIR is the only line that travels entirely above ground; the Tottenville stop is the southernmost subway stop in the city; and you only have to swipe your MetroCard at either the St. George or Tompkinsville stations.

to St. George and Tottenville

1   **St. George Ferry Terminal.** The ferry terminal was renovated a decade ago, and features design elements like a green roof, a pedestrian walkway to the Yankees stadium, and decorative fish tanks.

2   **Richmond County Bank Ballpark.** The minor-league Staten Island Yankees have called this stadium home since 2001, and regularly face off against other teams (including the Brooklyn Cyclones) during the summer.

3   **Pier 76.** Owned by the same family that runs Joe and Pat's, one of the most famous pizzerias in the city, this restaurant serves casual Italian fare, as well as incredibly delicious—and cheap—slices.

4   **Staten Island September 11 Memorial.** This elegant memorial, titled *Postcards,* overlooks the Manhattan skyline. It opened in 2004, and is inscribed with the name of every Staten Islander who died in the attacks.

5   **St. George Theatre.** This historic theater opened in 1929, but had become little more than a disused relic by the beginning of the 21st century. It finally reopened in 2004, and has since hosted Louis C.K., Joan Rivers, and more.

6   **Beso.** This tapas spot takes inspiration from regions across the globe for its menu, with dishes like Valencian paella, Cuban-style steak (served with fried plantains), and beef-and-manchego empanadas.

7   **Angelina's Ristorante.** There isn't much near the Tottenville stop, but there is this Italian eatery, located in an opulent home right next to the station. Traditional dishes can be enjoyed on one of the harbor-facing terraces.

8   **Conference House.** Built in the 17th century, this historic home was the site of a famous 1776 meeting between members of the Continental Congress (including Ben Franklin) and a representative for King George.

9   **National Lighthouse Museum.** In the works for more than a decade, this institution is located in a warehouse along the St. George waterfront, and serves as a hub for lighthouse history, education, and preservation.

SIR

5
FACTS
OFF THE

SIR

1. Conference House Park is actually the southernmost point in all of New York State.

2. For more than 200 years, a ferry ran between Tottenville and Perth Amboy, New Jersey, before stopping service in 1963.

3. The Outerbridge Crossing, connecting Staten Island and New Jersey, is named for former Port Authority chairman Eugenius Outerbridge.

4. Soon, the Atlantic and Nassau stations will be torn down to make way for one unified subway stop, called Arthur Kill.

5. The Staten Island Railway is the only subway line to use R44 cars, which have been in operation since 1973.

ALONG THE WAY

● **Tompkinsville**

● **Stapleton**

SIR

Flagship Brewing Company. Staten Island's first brewery in more than a decade has a tasting room and excellent beers.

5050 Skatepark. Both young and old daredevils flock to this skate park, a haven for BMX bikers, scooters, and skaters.

Grant City · New Dorp · Bay Terrace

High Rock Park. Part of the Staten Island Greenbelt, this park has many natural elements, including wetlands and ponds.

Jim Hanley's Universe. This outpost of the popular Manhattan shop stocks graphic novels, comic-book paraphernalia, and more.

Great Kills Park. Staten Island has many miles of beach, including four distinct areas within this waterfront park.

Index

EVENTS & PARADES

FINE DINING

FOOD & RESTAURANTS

Index

Index

Photo Credits

Images courtesy of New York City Department of Parks and Recreation, MTA Arts & Design, and the many generous and enthusiastic Flickr members who share a passion for seeking and celebrating the New York City that lies at the end of the line.

T=Top; TL=Top-Left; TM=Top-Middle; TR=Top-Right;
M=Middle; ML=Middle-Left; MR=Middle-Right
B=Bottom; BL=Bottom-Left; BM=Bottom-Middle; BR=Bottom-Right

BACK COVER

L to R / T to B